CLIMATE JUSTICE

A Call to Hope and Action

Edited by Pat Watkins

For all other requests, contact
Director of Transformative Education
United Methodist Women
475 Riverside Drive, Room 1501
New York, NY 10115
Phone: (212) 870-3745
Fax: (212) 870-3736

ISBN: 978-1-940182-28-5
Library of Congress Control Number: 2015948307

Cover and interior design: Rae Grant
Page production: Nanako Inoue
Cover image: Lucia Barreiros

Interior photos credited on page

Printed in the United States of America

United Methodist Women PURPOSE

The organized unit of United Methodist Women shall be a community of women whose purpose is to know God and to experience freedom as whole persons through Jesus Christ; to develop a creative, supportive fellowship; and to expand concepts of mission through participation in the global ministries of the church.

The Vision

Turning faith, hope and love into action on behalf of women, children and youth around the world.

Living the Vision

We provide opportunities and resources to grow spiritually, become more deeply rooted in Christ and put faith into action.

We are organized for growth, with flexible structures leading to effective witness and action.

We equip women and girls around the world to be leaders in communities, agencies, workplaces, governments and churches.

We work for justice through compassionate service and advocacy to change unfair policies and systems.

We provide educational experiences that lead to personal change in order to transform the world.

Table of Contents

Illustration of Earth as seen from the moon. The gravitational tug-of-war between earth and the moon raises a small bulge on the moon. The position of this bulge shifts slightly over time.
Image credit: NASA's Goddard Space Flight Center

Introduction

OF ALL THE THINGS the Apollo 8 astronauts could have chosen to read on Christmas Eve 1968 as they gazed back upon the earth as seen for the first time by human beings, they read Genesis 1:

> In the beginning when God created the heavens and the earth, the earth was a formless void and darkness covered the face of the deep, while a wind from God swept over the face of the waters. Then God said, "Let there be light"; and there was light. And God saw that the light was good; and God separated the light from the darkness. God called the light Day, and the darkness he called Night. And there was evening and there was morning, the first day.
>
> And God said, "Let there be a dome in the midst of the waters, and let it separate the waters from the waters." So God made the dome and separated the waters that were under the dome from the waters that were above the dome. And it was so. God called the dome Sky. And there was evening and there was morning, the second day.
>
> And God said, "Let the waters under the sky be gathered together into one place, and let the dry land appear." And it was so. God called the dry land Earth, and the waters that were gathered together he called Seas. And God saw that it was good. (Genesis 1:1–10)

For the first time in our history we were actually able to see the earth as a small blue planet in the midst of an incredibly vast universe. For the first time we could see just how fragile it seems and we knew it was all we have to call home.

It was no wonder these astronauts turned to the first creation story in the Bible. They were spiritually moved by what they saw. Even as they rode the wave of the most scientific and technologically advanced endeavor in human history, their minds turned to Genesis 1!

In the midst of ever-present injustices, the church has always been about seeking justice for all of earth's citizens. Perhaps that image of a small fragile earth hanging in blackness can help us realize the injustices that are being inflicted on the planet itself. The more we look into all of these injustices, the more we can see just how connected they are. We can never bring justice for God's people around the world until we bring justice to God's creation. And we will never be able to bring justice to the planet until we bring justice to all people. What we are doing to each other and what we are doing to God's creation are simply too interconnected. The worst part is that those who are responsible for causing the most harm to the planet suffer the fewest consequences and those least responsible for causing the harm suffer the most. What an injustice!

This study unpacks the complexities of that injustice and demonstrates just how complicated the solutions are. It also examines how we, as part of The United Methodist Church, can increase our understanding of those complexities and offer transformative solutions. Note the focus on climate *justice* in the title of this study rather than on climate change. Climate *in*justice is the result of climate change. Climate justice means setting right our relationships with each other *and* the earth, and the deeper we dig, the more we'll realize that we cannot do one without the other.

Chapter 1: A Biblical Theology of Creation Care

The Bible is full of references to relationships between God and people and people with each other—these are often discussed. We haven't spent as much time learning about another type of relationship found in the Bible, the one between God's people and God's creation. The author of this chapter, Pat Watkins, shows how many biblical stories speak to this relationship. Even some of the stories that are familiar to us, like what we learn about the Garden of Eden, Cain and Abel, and Noah and the flood, reveal amazing wisdom related to God's creation. There are dimensions of these stories about which we may not be very cognizant. The readers will almost certainly discover some new things about how we are to relate to God's creation in this chapter.

The Bible provides a witness to three kinds of relationships: our relationship with God, each other, and God's creation. These relationships are so interconnected that what happens to one affects the other two. In other words, when our relationship with God is abused, there are consequences for the land. Or when we treat each other with violence, the land suffers. It is the relationship of the relationships that is key here, both for understanding biblical wisdom and understanding what is happening today with regard to climate justice.

Chapter 2: A Biblical Model of Climate Justice

Rosemarie Wenner, author of Chapter 2, shares with us what the world would look like if we were to seriously put our faith into action and transform the world into the biblical vision of *shalom*: the restoration of right relationships. Drawing on biblical theology, John Wesley's understanding of a Christian relationship to creation, and the 2009 United Methodist Council of Bishop's document, "God's Renewed Creation," Wenner challenges us with a vision of holiness, not just for ourselves, but for all of God's creation.

Her holistic approach includes not just climate but also "our worldview, our spiritual practice, the worship life of our congregations, and our lifestyle," if we take seriously the theology of John Wesley. She speaks of prayer, of repentance, of the chasm between the way in which we live our lives in the West and the biblical and Wesleyan models. She speaks of the need for reconciliation, for a "lifestyle of humbleness," for learning how to live as "neither the owners nor the makers of the world," for the need to "practice not only personal holiness and social holiness, but also environmental holiness." What a vision! We pray that God will give us the strength to live into it.

Chapter 3: What Is Climate Justice? Why Is It a Religious Issue?

Climate justice is fundamentally and profoundly a religious issue. I. Malik Saafir, the author of Chapter 3, begins to explain why. He relates a story about happiness and unhappiness in which the ways people treat each other have very definite consequences on how we treat the earth. Happiness for some necessarily means unhappiness for others and for the earth. Happiness for all has to be the goal. The church has historically recognized that the ways in which we treat each other, particularly the ways in which we abuse each other, are fundamentally religious issues, and given the connections between our relationships with each other and our relationship with the earth, it just stands to reason that the ways we abuse God's creation also constitute a religious issue.

Saafir offers a new ending to the happiness story, one in which justice reigns, one that witnesses to the kin-dom[1] of God, one that celebrates a new creation. The Christ event offers reconciliation of all of our relationships, with God, each other, *and* creation. Solving our injustice issues will require that both humanity and creation are restored to the image of God. Climate justice is fundamentally and profoundly a religious issue. Until we all see it that way, we will not succeed in establishing justice.

Chapter 4: Climate Injustice: How Did We Get Here?

We have a tendency to simply live within the status quo, to accept whatever is happening to the planet as the inevitable reality of our time. But, that is not who we are as United Methodists! We are people of vision who are capable of transforming the world. To accomplish such a transformation, it is helpful to understand how we got ourselves into this mess in the first place. If we have a good understanding of how we arrived at our current situation, we will develop better tools to move forward in a different direction.

Jacqui Patterson, author of Chapter 4, helps us do just that. She doesn't mince words and she doesn't ease us into her chapter. Wealth, greed, the commoditization of labor and natural resources, colonization, the increasing gap between rich and poor, are all mentioned in the first two paragraphs. One of the saddest parts of our history is the way in which the institutional church has incorporated these Western values into our understanding of what it means to be Christian. Our task is even harder knowing that the church has failed to stand in opposition to a society saying we should acquire as much as we possibly can without regard for the consequent justice issues relating to God's people and God's creation.

Based on Patterson's understanding of how we got to where we are, systemic change will be necessary to solve our problems. "Now, in order to see real transformation, our challenge is to address the root causes of the climate crisis, including structural inequality, lack of real democracy, and the myopic pursuit of wealth through the commoditization of labor and natural resources." How will you be a part of such a transformation?

Chapter 5: Climate Injustice: Earth Consequences

Although the earth is able to put up with a great deal of abuse, it is showing significant signs of stress due to an inappropriate understanding of what it means to live in relationship with God's creation. Because our relationships with God and each other are not right, the earth suffers. Dottie Yunger, author of Chapter 5, is a scientist and a theologian, and therefore is in a perfect position to explain to us exactly how the earth is suffering. From learning the simple rules of living life on a barrier island off the coast of Belize so as not to damage the fragile coral reef that she was studying, to John Wesley's Three Simple Rules, Yunger weaves together her knowledge of science and theology in ways in which the reader can hear these two disciplines speaking to each other.

She explains what is happening to the earth scientifically in ways that all of us can understand. She discusses the benefits, both to humans and nonhumans, of healthy and well-functioning ecosystems and the consequences of abusing those systems. Perhaps by understanding the harm we are doing to creation, the rules we break, we may learn to do less harm. But the rules "need not be felt as onerous or burdensome; they are an invitation to live in relationship and abundant life with one another, with creation, and with God." Living a life of following the rules is a gift, not just to the earth, but also to ourselves.

Chapter 6: Climate Injustice: Human Consequences

Not only do our lifestyles have consequences for the earth itself, they also have consequences for humanity. We are so interconnected, humanity and the earth, that what befalls the earth befalls all of us. Chapter 6 looks at how we have abused our relationship with God's creation and how it has affected humanity. Author Norma Dollaga, who lives and works in the Philippines, shares stories of people who have suffered due to a suffering planet. The abuse of the earth in the name of profit by a mining company, for example, also abuses the poor, who are usually the ones living in proximity to some of the most environmentally devastated places on earth. Frighteningly, in the Philippines, there is risk, too, for those who speak out against environmental injustices.

Typhoons are normal and natural occurrences in the Philippines, Dollaga explains. But disasters have more to do with human vulnerability to those natural events. And human vulnerability has more to do with "bad government, unequal distribution of resources, lack of people's access to and control of the resources rightly belonging to them." Consequences to humanity are complex and complicated. Dollaga draws conclusions similar to Yunger's; caring for creation is a gift, enabling us to "live fully as human beings."

Chapter 7: Climate Justice: What Needs to Happen?

Kathleen Stone, author of Chapter 7, has the challenge of helping us understand what needs to happen in order for climate justice to become a reality in the world today. "The church needs to more powerfully model a way of doing it differently," she writes. This will entail not just focusing on the environment but also asking hard questions regarding financial profit, a growing economy, our independent way of thinking, and our understanding of efficiency.

In addition to asking the hard questions, the church is "uniquely situated to model the behaviors that are required in this time of needed urgent transformation." Stone cites presence, fellowship, worship, scripture, property, and money as tools with which the church can transform the world. She doesn't want us to merely make a difference; she wants us to actually solve some of the world's problems. And, Stone has the audacity to believe the church can do it as long as it is willing to take on the challenge.

Chapter 8: Climate Justice: How Can We Make It Happen?

Now that we have a vision of a transformed world, how can we, as individual United Methodists, as United Methodist Women members, districts, annual conferences, and as the church make this happen? More specifically, how can you, as a participant in this study, transform the world? You are a leader in the church, not just in your local congregation, but in your annual conference and beyond. How can you use your leadership to transform the world?

In Chapter 8, author Sharon Delgado, gives opportunities to bring about a "cultural shift." She, too, believes the church just may be in one of the best positions to do this. By citing work that is already being done by the General Board of Discipleship, United Methodist Women, the Council of Bishops, the General Board of Church and Society, the General Board of Global Ministries, the United Methodist Committee on Relief, and the General Board of Pensions and Health Benefits, Delgado gives us so much hope. She empowers us as leaders in the church to

Amazon River, Brazil. *Photo by Lucia Barreiros*

believe in ourselves and our ability to contribute to the solutions.

She also recognizes the complexities of the problems as she proclaims system change not climate change. Solutions have to involve international negotiations, market-based solutions, and building a global movement but the church gives her hope. We can do this!

Indeed, we do live on a small blue planet in the midst of a mind-bogglingly huge universe, a fragile planet, the only one we have to call home. And we believe that God had something to do with its creation, and continues to be in relationship with all that God has made. Our responsibility is to figure out how to live in right relationship with God, each other, and with the earth itself. Those Apollo 8 astronauts witnessed the first "earth rise." May the earth rise again in our hearts and minds through this study so that we can do justice to our God-given vocation of caring for the earth. ✪

Endnote

1. The phrase, *kin-dom of God*, was first coined by Ada Maria Isasi-Diaz. It emphasizes relationality, community, and equity as the basis of God's reign. It is an obvious contrast to systems of oppression and relations of domination.

A woman waters the crops at the Multi-Educational and Agricultural Jesuit Institute of Sudan (MAJIS), an agricultural school located outside Rumbek, South Sudan. *Photo by Paul Jeffrey*

Chapter 1

A Biblical Theology of Creation Care

Pat Watkins

IN THE GARDEN OF EDEN story, Adam was created out of the dust of the earth. "The Lord God formed the human from the topsoil of the fertile land and blew life's breath into his nostrils" (Genesis 2:7, CEB). The fact that we exist as living, breathing human beings suggests that we have a relationship with the earth because we were created out of it and we have a relationship with God because we breathe the very breath of the one who made us. God also created all the other animals out of the earth; hence we have a relationship with them since we were created out of the same "stuff." Scientists now know this to be true; the molecules that make up our bodies also make up the bodies of all other living creatures and are the same molecules that are found in the earth. We have a relationship with the earth because, quite literally, it is part of our DNA.

The earth, out of which we were made, is not just some stage upon which the salvation history of our scriptures is lived out. It is a living being in our story that, if ignored, will result in the loss of an accurate understanding of those scriptures. The land played an integral part of our story, from Genesis to Revelation. Recovering this understanding of the land in scripture is essential for us in the church to articulate a healthy and appropriate theology of creation care, as well as an appropriate response to concerns such as climate issues and other environmental problems.

Relationship with the land was integral to our creation *and* role in the garden; not only were we created out of the earth, we were placed in the garden to "farm it and to take care of it" (Genesis 2:15b, CEB). This is a vocation that set us apart from all the other creatures (none of them were assigned to care for creation) and one that defined our relationship with the earth—a relationship that would prove to have consequences if lived out improperly. Adam and Eve's sin is that they:

> …wanted the whole of creation to center upon them. Eating the forbidden fruit symbolized the human pretension at thinking that good and evil take their bearing from self-interest and desire. Anthropocentrism, the refusal to understand ourselves as but one part of a larger created whole, is the central sin. Alienation from nature, symbolized in the expulsion from the garden, is the necessary consequence.[1]

"Cursed is the ground because of you; in pain you will eat from it every day of your life. Weeds and thistles will grow for you, even as you eat the field's plants" (Genesis 3:17b–18, CEB). We didn't lose our relationship with the earth as a result of our disobedience, but it became a far more difficult relationship, replete with weeds and thistles and pain and sweat. Unfortunately, using Roundup® to deal with the weeds and thistles is not enough to redeem our God-given relationship with the land.

Cain and Abel's story also exemplifies this theology. God made it clear to Cain that there are parameters within which Cain was to live life. "If you do the right thing, won't you be accepted? But if you don't do the right thing, sin will be waiting at the door ready to strike! It will entice you, but you must rule over it" (Genesis 4:7, CEB). But Cain, just like his father Adam, chose a different direction. He chose not to live within the parameters God defined for him, and killed his brother Abel.

It is ironic that Cain chose to kill Abel on Cain's farm, the land that Cain knew and loved, the land with which he had an intimate relationship. In fact, it was the land itself that indicted Cain to God. "'What did you do?' asked God. 'The voice of your brother's blood is crying to me from the ground that opened its mouth to take your brother's blood from your hand'" (Genesis 4:10–11, CEB). The land, here, is a living character in this story. Again, just like Adam, Cain has to suffer the consequences of his disobedience—his decision to refuse to see himself as part of a larger family. Listen to God's punishment: "When you farm the fertile land, it will no longer grow anything for you, and you will become a roving nomad on the earth" (Genesis 4:12, CEB).

For most of us that punishment might not sound so severe; we have chosen to be "roving nomads on the earth." We chase careers all over the place rather than choosing to root ourselves on a particular piece of land or even in a particular community. But for Cain, one who was rooted to a specific geographical place and to a specific, God-given vocation, farming, God's punishment was, "more than I can bear. Now that you've driven me away from the fertile land and I am hidden from your presence, I'm about to become a roving nomad on the earth, and anyone who finds me will kill me" (Genesis 4:13b–14). For Cain to lose his vocation, his relationship with the land, was to be hidden from the presence of

God—at least from his perspective. His relationship with the land and his relationship with God were so intertwined for Cain that the loss of one meant the loss of the other.

Our relationships with God, each other, and the earth are so intimately connected in the Old Testament that not one of these three relationships can exist apart from the other two. Cain's loss of his relationship with the land, and subsequent hiddenness from the presence of God, gave him the false belief that his life was in danger because of what he had done. But no matter how we perceive our relationship with God, God stays true to us; in Cain's case, God placed a mark on his forehead, not for condemnation, but for protection. This is the first story of redemption in the Bible!

In the Garden of Eden and the story of Cain and Abel, the consequence of disobedience led to a damaged relationship with God's creation: in Adam's case, a curse on the ground; in Cain's case, a curse of being separated from the land that he knows and loves. Clearly, our decisions and choices in life often have direct consequences in terms, not only of our relationships with each other and God, but also with God's creation. At no point in history is this more evident than today in the midst of the climate crisis in which we find ourselves.

Over the last two hundred years we have made decisions that we thought were in our best interest but instead caused untold suffering for the planet and for those whose day-to-day existence depends on an intimate relationship with the earth—the very ones least responsible for the problems our decisions caused. Like Cain and Adam before him, we cannot undo our actions of the past, we can only move forward. The key for us as a church is to decide how to move ahead in ways that are healing and redemptive for God's creation. As we discover how to do this ministry of creation care, we just might discover that our relationships with each other, particularly our sisters and brothers in developing countries, and our relationship with God may very well be enhanced—perhaps even redeemed.

When we think of the Noah story, we think of the ark, a bunch of animals, the flood, and the rainbow. We seldom remember the very beginning of the story. On the day that Noah was born, his father, Lamech, who was so full of hope for his son, said, "This one will give us relief from our hard work, from the pain in our hands, because of the fertile land that the Lord cursed" (Genesis 5:29, CEB). Because of Noah's righteousness, maybe *he* would be the one to reverse the curse brought about by Adam and Cain!

It is hard to find a direct connection between the disobedience of Adam and Cain with the consequent curse of the land, and the evil and violence and corruption that seemed to fill the earth in Noah's day; however, it is clear that the violence with which Cain treated his brother directly resulted in the degradation of the earth itself. So, it follows that the violence and corruption that motivated God to do something about it may very well have been connected to a loss of an appropriate relationship with the land. Clearly, the order that God brought to creation in Genesis 1 was nowhere to be found, at least within the human population. God regretted ever creating us!

Another part of the Noah story that we may not remember comes near the end. After the flood was over the waters receded and the ark came to rest on dry ground. All the animals exited the ark and God put a rainbow in the sky as a sign of the covenant that God would never again destroy the earth by flood. The part that does not get much attention is whom God made the covenant with. We assume, rightly so, that the covenant was made with Noah. In fact it was with Noah, his family, and his descendants (including you and me), and it was also made between God and "every living thing with you on behalf of every future generation" (Genesis 9:12, CEB). God's covenant was also with the animals on the ark and all of *their* future generations and even between God and the earth itself! (Genesis 9:13, CEB)

God's covenant with the earth restored a right relationship between humanity, God, and God's creation. After everything settled down, Noah returned to the original vocation God gave to Adam, to "serve and keep" the garden. Noah was a farmer. Perhaps his righteousness was somehow couched in his ability, not only to be obedient to God, but also to exercise a right relationship with creation.

There are threads running through all three of these stories, the Garden of Eden, Cain and Abel, and Noah, that unmistakably connect human obedience, disobedience, and righteousness with how we relate to God, each other, and the earth. Climate injustice is a symptom that these relationships are not right today.

In very simplistic terms, the rest of the Old Testament and all of the New Testament depict God's work to restore these relationships to rightness again. In Leviticus, God declares, "The land must not be permanently sold because the land is mine" (Leviticus 25:23, CEB). Psalm 24 declares, "The earth is the Lord's and everything in it, the world and its inhabitants too" (Psalm 24:1, CEB). Creation was never given to us to do with as we please, not even as a gift. Creation belongs to God; it always has and always will be God's. One of our current sins is that we believe creation exists to serve us; that exploitation of creation will make us wealthy. In fact, according to the vocation given to Adam, we are to serve creation, a creation that belongs solely to God.

God even helps define our relationship with the land. Every seven years the land is to rest, to enjoy a Sabbath. The farmers were instructed not to plant in the seventh year:

> You will plant your fields for six years, and prune your vineyards and gather their crops for six years. But in the seventh year the land will have a special Sabbath rest, a Sabbath to the Lord: you must not plant your fields or prune your vineyards. You must not harvest the secondary growth of your produce or gather the grapes of your freely growing vines. It will be a year of special rest for the land. (Leviticus 25:3–5, CEB)

The connection between relationship with each other, especially the poor and those on the margins, and relationship with God's creation is clearly delineated in the texts about gleaning. From Deuteronomy:

> Whenever you are reaping the harvest of your field and you leave some grain in the field, don't go back and get it. Let it go to the immigrants, the orphans, and the widows so that the Lord your God blesses you in all that you do. Similarly, when you beat the olives off your olive trees, don't go back over them twice. Let the leftovers go to the immigrants, the orphans, and the widows. Again, when you pick the grapes of your vineyard, don't pick them over twice. Let the leftovers go to the immigrants, the orphans, and the widows. Remember how you were a slave in Egypt. That's why I am commanding you to do this thing. (Deuteronomy 24:19–22, CEB)

God is commanding the farmers to alter their relationship with the land and to alter their understanding of a system of economy that encourages us to "get all we can" in order to care for the poor. Maintaining a right relationship with each other, especially those on the margins, is directly related to how we choose to interact with the land. The farmers could have harvested everything and made more money. But God is essentially saying, "But that is not how you are to live if you are in a relationship with me." Being in relationship with

God changes how we relate to each other and with the land.

Unfortunately, we have not always paid attention to God's commands. As Israel's history unfolded, we forgot the God-ordained balancing of those three relationships. The sin God was trying so hard to prevent in us was the sin of believing creation exists solely to serve us. It is our sin today and it is the sin of God's people throughout history.

Amos and Hosea were eighth-century prophets who were witnessing a cultural, ethical, and economic shift in the life of Israel. The shift was away from small-scale and subsistence agriculture to a centralized, agri-business model. Royal families began to see the economic advantages of international trade; consequently, they did two things. First, they forced the farmers to shift production away from crops that fed people, the farmers' families included, and toward cash crops like grain, olive oil, and wine. Second, they taxed farmers more and more heavily in the form of these products of agriculture. That meant there was less and less land to feed the people. In bad years, many farmers went into debt to support themselves and their families, putting up their land as collateral. Many lost their land as a result, which was fine for the people at the top, who began hiring laborers at low wages to work the land to make the profits of international trade even higher. Life was great for this new, rich, landowning aristocracy; even the religious leaders endorsed the policies of the state that resulted in increasing the gap between the rich and the poor. Not so for the farmers who were bearing the brunt of the burdens. Abuse of the poor and abuse of the land go hand in hand when it comes to lining the pockets of the rich. And, given the biblical witness, we've been at it for a long time.

Biblical archaeology has confirmed this interpretation as archaeologists have discovered larger houses, large pits for storing grain, regional store-houses for wine and oil, terracing and irrigation for orchards and vineyards, even containers for oil and wine identified as belonging to certain royal families.[2]

Amos and Hosea simply could not remain silent in the face of such injustice. Amos focused mainly on the economic inequalities, the corruption in the marketplaces, and the abuse of the poor on the part of the rich:

> Hear this, you who trample on the needy and destroy the poor of the land, saying, "When will the new moon be over so that we may sell grain, and the Sabbath so that we may offer wheat for sale, make the ephah smaller, enlarge the shekel, and deceive with false balances, in order to buy the needy for silver and the help-less for sandals, and sell garbage as grain?" (Amos 8:4–6, CEB)

Hosea was able to connect the abuse of our rela-tionships with each other and God with the con-sequences to the earth itself. Again, relationship with God, each other, and the land are so inter-twined in Old Testament Israelite culture that a change in the balance of any of the three results in problems with the other two:

> Hear the Lord's word, people of Israel; for the Lord has a dispute with 'he inhabitants of the land. There's no faithful love or loyalty, and no knowledge of God in the land. Swearing, lying, murder, together with stealing and adultery are common; bloody crime followed by bloody crime. Therefore the earth itself becomes sick, and all who live on it grow weak; together with the wild animals and the birds in the sky, even the fish of the sea are dying. (Hosea 4:1–3, CEB)

These words, in particular, have an eerie ring of truth today. We know firsthand that abusing our relationships with each other results in negative consequences to the earth and vice versa. Cli-mate change is a perfect example of this. How can we have a healthy relationship with God if we abuse either God's people or God's creation? As in Old Testament days, these relationships with God, each other, and the earth are just as intertwined today. Perhaps one thing that makes today more devastating is that so many people are not aware of the connections between these relationships. We can't ask forgiveness and be motivated to change if we're not even aware of the problems and/or our complicity with them.

The Old Testament is not our only source of scriptural wisdom. The writer of John's Gospel believes Jesus was present with God at creation and that he had a part in the creation of all that has ever come into existence. "The Word was with God in the beginning. Everything came into being through the Word, and without the Word nothing came into being" (John 1:2–3, CEB). We have a tendency to gloss over the sig-nificance of what John was trying to help us un-derstand in these opening verses. But, Norman Wirzba, author and theology and ecology pro-fessor, sees them as defining the activity of God in Christ:

> The character of creation, its meaning and its hope, was thus redefined in terms of the activ-ity of God in Jesus Christ. God's intention in creation, we might say, now finds its definitive focus in the work of this man. If we want to know as completely as possible what it is for creation to be creation, we must look at the life of Jesus Christ.[3]

This "cosmic" understanding of the coming of Christ and his work on earth is reflected in John 3:16, "God so loved the world that he gave his only Son, so that everyone who believes in him won't perish but will have eternal life" (CEB). The Greek word for "world" in this scripture is per-haps more accurately translated "cosmos." God so loved, not just the people on earth, but the en-tirety of God's creation that God sent Jesus to live among us.

Paul follows suit, believing Jesus to be the redeemer, not just of humanity, but also of all creation. Everything that has ever come into existence is subject to the redeeming love of God in Christ: "Because all the fullness of God was pleased to live in him, and he reconciled all things to himself through him, whether things on earth or in the heavens. He brought peace through the blood of his cross" (Colossians 1:19–20, CEB). Could the mission of Christ, and hence the mission of the church, be the renewing of all things? And if so, what role could and should the church play in the renewing of creation? We pray for God's kin-dom to come *on earth* as it is in heaven. How does this understanding transform our ways of interacting with and being in relationship with the earth?

Almost all of Jesus' parables had to do with the natural world. This fact does not make him a left-wing environmentalist, but it does speak to the culture of his day. He knew that by telling stories about farming or shepherding or fields or fishing, people would understand what he was talking about, simply because his audience was so connected to the earth themselves. In other words, Jesus was depending upon the relationship between the people and the earth to teach what he needed to teach. The entire culture in which Jesus lived, preached, healed, and taught was agrarian. Everyone, with the exception of perhaps a very small minority of royal families, was intimately connected to the land.

For example, the parable of the sower in Luke 8:4–15 is a story about a farmer who sows seed on a path, among rocks, in weeds, and in good soil. Everybody who heard Jesus tell this story knew that the seed sowed in good soil was the seed that would sprout and produce a plant. But due to our disconnection with the earth, especially those of us in more affluent countries, this parable is losing its significance. People who have never planted seeds, children who think their food comes from the grocery store, those who have never even dug into the earth with their hands are all at risk of entirely missing the point of this parable. I used to work with a young woman in her mid-twenties with a master's degree who didn't know potatoes grew underground until I told her. Our increased isolation from God's creation will accompany a decreased understanding of much of the wisdom of Jesus' teachings.

Similarly, Jesus used natural imagery to describe himself to us, for example, likening himself to a shepherd or a vine. He knew his hearers would understand what he was talking about. And ultimately, he chose ordinary elements of the earth to represent himself in what became a sacrament of the church, the Lord's Supper. He could have chosen gold or silver or some precious stone to represent himself to us. He could have commissioned an artist to carve an elaborate wooden carving to represent himself to us. But instead, Jesus chose everyday elements of the earth, bread and wine. The symbolism of his choice was significant both to demonstrate just how personally available he was choosing to be to all of us, and also significant relative to his relationship with creation, and hopefully, ours as well.

It follows that if the whole Christ event actually includes creation, then the church's role is not just to become "green" because everybody else is doing it; the church's role is to incorporate caring for God's creation into every dimension of our ministry and mission in The United Methodist Church. Creation care, as defined by biblical theology, is part and parcel of what it means to be disciples of Jesus Christ. It is not optional, just for a handful of us who care; it is at the very heart and soul of the mission of the church. It is for all of us who claim to be Christian!

The prophets were fairly clear in making connections between our relationship with the land and the justice or injustice with which we treat each other, particularly how those in power and the wealthy treat those who have no power, who might even be oppressed, and who are poor. The wealthy can take the land from the poor, whether by force, or by a decree or with a check. With land comes power, the ability to then employ the poor for starvation wages. The rich become rich *because* the poor remain poor. This increasing gap between rich and poor is not coincidental. And, amazingly, this dynamic that we know exists today also existed in ancient Israel. Justice, as it incorporates treatment of each other and treatment of the land, is as old as God's people.

Climate justice may be a different and new manifestation of this dynamic, but the basics are not new. The ways in which the wealthy, in general, have treated the earth include exploitation for personal financial gain and personal comfort and luxury, without regard to the consequences such as pollution, global warming, toxic dumps, etc. This exploitation goes hand-in-hand with the exploitation of the poor at the hands of the wealthy. The poor of the world have to live with the effects of the damage those of us in the West have perpetrated on the earth. It all started with environmental racism, the location of our toxic industries and waste dumps in neighborhoods of color, and it has progressed to climate change being caused primarily by the wealthy nations, the consequences being suffered by the poor in other parts of the world, many times without awareness and sometimes without regard on the part of the wealthy nations.

Gus Speth, former dean of the School of Forestry and Environmental Studies at Yale University, addressed a group of religious leaders several years ago:

> I used to think the top environmental problems facing the world were global warming, environmental degradation and ecosystem collapse, and that we scientists could fix those problems with enough science, but I was wrong. The real problem is not those three items but greed, selfishness, and apathy. And for that we need a spiritual and cultural transformation. And we scientists don't know how to do that. We need your help.[4]

Speth is talking to you, a leader in The United Methodist Church! You may not be a climate scientist and, in fact, the Bible does not specifically mention "climate justice," but it has a great deal to say about greed, selfishness, and apathy. The ways in which we live our lives today are reflected in the scriptures, from Adam and Eve selfishly choosing to be "more" than what God had in mind for them, to Cain's disobedience of God and horrible abuse of his relationship with his brother, to the royal families and wealthy landowners greedily taking advantage of the poor, to Jesus' parables and teachings about wealth and exploitation of the poor. No, you may not be a climate scientist, but you are a Christian, a United Methodist Christian, and you have the responsibility, in living out your discipleship, not just to care for God's creation, but to transform The United Methodist Church, which will then lead to the transformation of the world! ✪

Endnotes

1. Norman Wirzba, *The Paradise of God* (Oxford, U.K.: Oxford University Press, 2003), 133–134.

2. Ellen Davis, *Scripture, Culture, and Agriculture* (New York: Cambridge University Press, 2009), 122–124.

3. Norman Wirzba, *The Paradise of God*, 48.

4. Duane Elgin, "Why Climate Change Requires a Consciousness Change," Huffpost Healthy Living, *The Huffington Post*, updated August 20, 2011, www.huffingtonpost.com/duane-elgin/climate-change-consciousness_b_879581.html.

An elephant passing by the north side of Mount Kilimanjaro in Kenya. *Photo by Charles Asik*

About the Author

The Reverend Pat Watkins is the first, and currently only, General Board of Global Ministries missionary assigned to the care of God's creation. An ordained elder of the Virginia Annual Conference, Watkins has served churches in Virginia; been a missionary in Nigeria; was the environmental policy advisor for the Virginia Interfaith Center for Public Policy; and served as the executive director of Virginia Interfaith Power and Light, and as a church and community worker as the executive director of Caretakers of God's Creation, a creation care ministry of the Virginia Conference. In his current role, Watkins' tasks are to implement a national United Methodist creation care ministry for the United States, encourage all U.S. annual conferences to establish creation care ministries, work with the United Methodist Council of Bishops regarding their 2009 document "God's Renewed Creation," and establish and work with a Global Ministries creation care team to organize creation care ministries throughout the world.

Worship, "A Sojourn to Sacredness," Virginia Conference of The United Methodist Church, 2011.
Photo by Pat Watkins

Chapter 2

A Biblical Model of Climate Justice

Rosemarie Wenner

WHILE I WAS REFLECTING on the task of writing on the theme "A Biblical Model of Climate Justice," I was on an eight-day hike in a mountainous area in my home country, Germany. What a peaceful place! And what a great creation! I was reminded of Psalm 104:

> From your lofty house, you water the mountains. The earth is filled full by the fruit of what you've done. You make grass grow for the cattle; you make plants for human farming in order to get food from the ground . . . The Lord's trees are well watered—the cedars of Lebanon, which God planted, where the birds make their nests, where the stork has a home in the cypresses . . . Lord, you have done so many things! You made them all so wisely! (Psalm 104:13–14; 16–17; 24a, CEB)

But even in the beautiful nature of Germany, a rather safe and secure country in Middle Europe, I observed signs of the devastation caused by Cyclone Kyrill. this storm downed thousands of trees all over Europe from January 18–19, 2007. No doubt, we live under much better conditions than people in many parts of the earth. However, even in Germany one starts to talk of climate change in a rather existential way. There have already been two so-called century floods in the last few years. Sadly enough, those who are most in danger because of floods, drought, or rising sea levels live in far poorer parts of the world than I. The "Minute on Climate Justice,"

adopted November 8, 2013, at the Tenth Assembly of the World Council of Churches reads:

> Victims of climate change are the new face of the poor, the widow and the stranger that are especially loved and cared for by God (Deut. 10:17–18). When creation is threatened in this way, churches are called to speak out and act as an expression of their commitment to life, justice and peace.[1]

Doing everything possible to diminish the speed of climate change is an act of justice toward marginalized people and toward future generations. There is an urgency to work for climate justice in the twenty-first century. But, this seems to be a rather new phenomenon and a challenge that was not obvious in biblical times. Are there references to our theme in the Holy Scriptures of the Hebrew and Christian Bible? Oh, yes, there are, although people lived under completely different circumstances and with fewer possibilities to exploit natural resources and to pollute the air. Let me briefly describe four approaches:

"In the beginning God created the heavens and the earth."—Genesis 1:1

The first chapters of the Bible offer two stories, told in two different times, both putting into a narrative what we confess in the Apostle's Creed: "I believe in God, the Father almighty, creator of heaven and earth."[2] The first (and younger) creation account in Genesis 1–2:3 states that all that is was made by God. God saw what was made and it was all good. The second creation account in Genesis 2:4–25 tells us that God created the garden as a living organism. Everything was pleasant. Both stories underline that we—the humans—are also created by God. The stories of creation show how we are a part of the whole, and yet we are unique because of our responsibility.

In the older account in Genesis 2, the human named all the livestock, birds, and wild animals. Naming is a powerful act of describing and relationship building. It can easily be misused as an annexation. The newer story in Genesis 1–2:3 reads:

> God blessed them and said to them [Adam and Eve], "Be fertile and multiply; fill the earth and master it. Take charge of the fish of the sea, the birds of the sky, and everything crawling on the ground . . . I now give to you all the plants on the earth that yield seeds and all the trees whose fruits produce its seeds within it. These will be your food." (Genesis 1:28–29, CEB)

In regards to human accountability for the natural resources, the creation accounts have had a rather difficult history of reception. Some have interpreted the fact that humankind has an exceptional role to play as an invitation to use creation mainly in their own interests. As a result, the exploitation of creation became common practice, particularly in regions where Christianity was the main religion. And this is true even today, although in the last decades we have spoken of our responsibility to care for the creation. We take care, unless we have to sacrifice our comfort or the welfare of our economy.

To work toward climate justice, we have to reread the creation stories. Let us read them as stories that tell us how we as human beings are part of the whole, interwoven in the circles of life, dependent upon the grace and creativity of God

who made heaven and earth and all of us. Yes, we are called to master the earth. But we have to copy the care and the love of the Holy One who has created the whole, including us. We need a healthy balance of the two tasks "to till" and "to keep" (Genesis 2:15) to learn how to use and not to misuse what God created; rejoicing in what was made is a strong motivation.

"The earth is full of your creations!"
—Psalm 104:24b, CEB

Psalm 104 is a marvelous poem praising God and God's creation. Indeed, there is a network of life, all species have a unique part in it, and the earth in its beauty is a living praise for God. Living into a spirituality that values and honors God's gift is a model for people who want to change their lifestyle and work toward climate justice. We can hardly read this psalm without changing our attitude about using natural resources. The air that we breathe is a sign of life. Clean water is a source for renewal. The little bird and the big deer are co-creatures. Together with the sun, moon, earth, fire, hail, mountains, and animals we as humans are invited to praise the Lord: "Lord, my God, how fantastic you are!" (Psalm 104:1). In the New Testament, we find an old hymn in Colossians 1:15–20. The young church praises Christ as the one who is first over all creation. By Christ, all things were created and all things are held together in him (verses 16–17). This old prayer worships Christ as the one in whom everything is held together and in whom all things are reconciled (verse 20). John Wesley went so far as to see Christ in all that is:

> [Christ] is now the life of everything that lives in any kind or degree. He is the source of the lowest species of life, that of vegetables; as being the source of all the motion on which vegetation depends. He is the fountain of the life of animals, the power by which the heart beats, and the circulating juices flow. He is the fountain of all the life that man possesses in common with other animals.[3]

If we see Christ in all that is created and if we understand ourselves as a part of the family of nature, it will impact our worldview, our spiritual practice, the worship life of our congregations, and our lifestyle.

Throughout history, we find role models for spiritual practices that help us to see the world with eyes of admiration, joy, and gratitude for all of God's gifts. Francis from Assisi spoke of "Mother Earth," "Brother Sun," and "Sister Water." Such an attitude of awe for the natural world is also typical of Native American traditions as well as of Asian and African cultures. When the Council of Bishops of The United Methodist Church offered its document "God's Renewed Creation: Call to Hope and Action" to the church in 2009, it invited the people called United Methodist to receive the pastoral letter in a liturgical form. In a spirit of prayer, we may repent of our selfishness to be transformed to praise God by prayers, hymns, and actions of hope.

"Then I saw a new heaven and a new earth" —Revelation 21:1a, CEB

In the last pages of the Bible, we read the equivalent of the beginning. John, the author of the book of Revelation, tells us his vision of the new heaven and the new earth created by God, who made this earth and who continues to make all things new. An image for the new world is the new city of Jerusalem, a city of glory, where justice and peace kiss one another, where nobody has to suffer, no wiping of tears, no terror, no illness, no death. And in his vision John even sees a river of life-giving water, with the tree of life at each side of the water. Here is the garden that was mentioned in the oldest story of how God created the world. At the end of the days, God finishes what God began. This is the great vision we live with.

Unfortunately, many Christians read this vision as a story of devastation. The old world comes to an end. In fact, this is a biblical statement. And there are many apocalyptic descriptions in the Bible, particularly in Revelation, of how that end might cause pain and chaos. We have to ask ourselves, however, whether those statements must be interpreted as a description of what's going to happen or as a wake-up call to repent and to change our lifestyles. Many Christians live with the first interpretation. This world will come to an end; therefore the main emphasis is to save souls. The exploitation of the earth and the resulting injustices that occur as consequences of climate change are seen as an expression of the sinful nature of humankind that leads to the destruction of the world.

Such an approach is not Wesleyan and it is not biblical. If we believe in Christ, risen from death in order to renew us and to make all things new, we are called to give space for God's grace—transforming us so that we can transform the world. The aim of God is not devastation, but new life in continuation of God's great redemptive and restorative action when Christ was resurrected from death to life. We, therefore, are called to dream God's dream of the new heaven and the new earth and to serve as God's coworkers by acting with hope toward change for the better, according to God's aim of peace, justice, and reconciliation.

In its pastoral letter, the Council of Bishops of The United Methodist Church writes:

> As people in the tradition of John Wesley, we understand reconciliation and renewal to be part of the process of salvation that is already under way. We are not hemmed in to a fallen world. Rather, we are part of a divine unfolding process to which we must contribute. As we faithfully respond to God's grace and call to action, the Holy Spirit guides us in this renewal. With a resurrection spirit, we look forward to the renewal of the whole creation and commit ourselves to that vision. We pray that God will

accept and use our lives and resources that we rededicate to a ministry of peace, justice, and hope to overcome poverty and disease, environmental degradation, and the proliferation of weapons and violence.[4]

"... good stewards of the manifold grace of God ..." —1 Peter 4:10b

As a people who confess "the earth is the Lord's and everything in it" (Psalm 24:1a, CEB) and who worship God, the creator, full of hope that God will create a new heaven and a new earth, we have to learn how to live as a part of the creation in a sustainable and responsible way. The biblical model for such a lifestyle can be called stewardship. We are neither the owners nor the makers of the world. While we are honored to play an important role in making best use of God's gifts including all the natural resources, we also have to accept our responsibility.

God, the creator and owner of the world, wants life for all with a fair sharing of the natural gifts among all people and a supportive coexistence with the whole creation. Just as any employee has to accept the will of his or her boss, we as stewards have to make use of the world and relate to our fellow creatures in a way that pleases God. John Wesley described stewardship as such:

> We are now God's stewards. We are indebted to him for all we have. . . . A steward is not at liberty to use what is lodged in his hand as he pleases but as his master pleases. . . . He is not the owner of any of these things but barely entrusted with them by another. . . . Now this is exactly the case of everyone with relation to God. We are not at liberty to use what God has lodged in our hands as we please, but as God pleases, who alone is the possessor of heaven and earth and the Lord of every creature.[5]

As good stewards, we have to seek for justice for all. We have to learn the virtue of humility to check our needs according to the biblical advice: "But if we have food and clothing, we will be content with these" (1 Timothy 6:8). Good stewards trust that God provides plenty for everyone. Therefore, we will learn to overcome the greed of getting more and more just to satisfy the ambition to receive as much as possible. This lifestyle of humbleness is difficult to practice, because it is countercultural in a world where "growth" means constant increase of wealth, regardless of the costs. Learning a lifestyle of "enough" demands a spiritual practice of openness for the guidance of the Holy Spirit.

As Christians, we are neither defined by the things we possess nor by the wealth that we achieve. We are defined by our relationship to Christ and through Christ to the whole creation. With this foundation, we learn to live toward the kin-dom of God, although we are still citizens of earth. We will be richly blessed when we choose to live this way. And the blessings will extend far beyond ourselves to our children and grandchildren when we are good stewards of God's creation. We will reap what we sow. If we pollute the air, it will not only affect the poor in other parts of the world, it will also come back to us. Our care for nature will preserve it for our well-being as well as for the good of others. Learning how to please God will please us as well!

Acting on the Words

At the end of the Sermon on the Mount, Jesus encourages his disciples to put his words into action: "Everybody who hears these words of mine and puts them into practice is like a wise builder who built a house on bedrock" (Matthew 7:24, CEB). Our current environmental conditions literally cause storms and floods. We should be wise and practice what we have learned.

It is time to practice not only personal holiness and social holiness, but also environmental holiness. This is the term used by the bishops in their pastoral letter, "God's Renewed Creation."

Martha Yar uses a hoe to prepare the ground for planting at the Multi-Educational and Agricultural Jesuit Institute of Sudan (MAJIS), an agricultural school located outside Rumbek, South Sudan.
Photo by Paul Jeffrey

There are several dimensions of environmental holiness. Every single person can start by asking key questions: What do I really need? Where do I buy what I need? What am I eating? How do I go from here to there? Is there an alternative way to get there other than by car or plane? How do I compensate for the carbon dioxide that I have used? All these are rather small contributions. Compared with the huge environmental damage that has already taken place it is almost nothing. However, there is an African proverb, "Many little people, in many little places, taking many little steps, can change the face of the world." Environmental holiness also means that we need to reflect on our church life. We bishops committed ourselves "to measure the 'carbon footprint' of our

Episcopal and denominational offices, determine how to reduce it, and implement those changes." And we also pledged: "We will urge our congregations, schools, and settings of ministry to do the same."[6] It takes time to collect all the necessary statistics and to look for concrete options to inspire others to follow the example. And, at the same time, an examination of our carbon footprints will help to raise our awareness of the potential negative consequences of the work we do and add to our motivation to work for change within our own lives, the lives of our churches, and in our policies.

What is most important: All of us can build coalitions with people of good will to work for the necessary political and economic changes. This is the most difficult part of the journey. Too many people speak of the impossibility of change. Politicians and corporate leaders often cite that there are no alternatives when they are asked to change. But for people of faith, there is always the alternative to repent and develop healthier and more sustainable options. By God's grace we will learn how to do better in tilling *and* keeping the earth.

A strong source of inspiration to do all of this is the joy we experience from God's beautiful creation. We need liturgical practices that raise our awareness of the richness of God's creation and our responsibility to it. One of the most successful ecumenical programs in Germany is the "Ecumenical Day of Creation" on the first Friday in September. Each year there is a national event planned by the National Council of Churches and copied by many regional and local ecumenical councils. We give thanks to God for creation, and commit ourselves anew to work toward sustainability to preserve God's gifts for future generations.

The pastoral letter, "God's Renewed Creation" ends with a blessing. Because we trust in God, we trust in a future with hope. Therefore:

> May God's grace purify our reason, strengthen our will, and guide our action. May the love of God, the peace of Christ, and the power of the Holy Spirit be among you, everywhere and always, so that you may be a blessing to all creation and to all the children of God, making peace, nurturing and practicing hope, choosing life and coming to life eternal. Amen.[7] ✿

Endnotes

1. "Minute on Climate Justice," World Council of Churches, 10th Assembly, October 30–November 8, 2014, Busan, Republic of Korea.

2. "The Apostles Creed, Traditional Version," *The United Methodist Hymnal* (Nashville: Abingdon Press, 1989), 881.

3. John Wesley, Sermon 77, "Spiritual Worship," *The Sermons of John Wesley*, General Board of Global Ministries of The United Methodist Church, www.umcmission.org/Find-Resources/ John-Wesley-Sermons/Sermon-77-Spiritual-Worship, II:3.

4. United Methodist Council of Bishops, "God's Renewed Creation: Call to Hope and Action," Pastoral Letter, 2009, http://hopeandaction.org/main/wp-content/uploads/2010/03/Pastoral-Letter-Eng-Handout-2-col.pdf.

5. John Wesley, Sermon 51, "The Good Steward," *The Sermons of John Wesley*, General Board of Global Ministries of The United Methodist Church, www.umcmission.org/Find-Resources/ John-Wesley-Sermons/Sermon-51-The-Good-Steward, I:1.

6. United Methodist Council of Bishops, "God's Renewed Creation: Call to Hope and Action."

7. Ibid.

About the Author

Bishop Rosemarie Wenner was born and raised in Eppingen, Germany, where she was nurtured by a small United Methodist congregation in Southern Germany. She studied at the United Methodist Theological Seminary in Reutlingen and served as pastor of congregations in Karlsruhe-Durlach, Hockenheim, and Darmstadt-Sprendlingen before her appointment as superintendent of the Frankfurt District in 1996.

In February 2005, she was elected bishop at the Germany Central Conference in Wuppertal. Wenner is the first woman elected to the United Methodist episcopacy outside of the United States.

Wenner is married to Tobias Wenner and they live in Nussloch, Germany.

Sunset landscape and giraffe in Serengeti National Park in Tanzania, East Africa.
Photo by Mark52Canada

Chapter 3

What Is Climate Justice? Why Is It a Religious Issue?

I. Malik Saafir

And God saw everything that God had made, and indeed, it was very good. —Genesis 1:31a

My understanding of environmental stewardship began when I enlisted in the United States Navy (USN). As we set sail for the Mediterranean Sea, I watched as the Virginia shoreline diminished and I discovered the expanding horizon of the Atlantic Ocean. This moment revealed that the size and depth of the Atlantic Ocean and earth are beyond my human comprehension. I discovered the interconnectedness of all species living in water and on land.

I also drew from my childhood experiences of fishing in the local creeks and ponds to understand environmental stewardship. My childhood was full of adventures, setting out each day to perfect the art of fishing with family and friends in Fourche Creek in Little Rock, Arkansas. As a novice fisherman, I discovered the anatomy of fish and their dependence on clean water and other species to survive. I witnessed how each species of fish lived off other living organisms in the water and how I, in turn, lived off the fish.

As a sailor, I also witnessed how we shared the sea with other animals and marine organisms, as well as our continued destruction of the ocean's ecosystem from pollution. Each day at sea, I saw plastic and other non-biodegradable trash floating in the ocean. This called me to

question the amount of waste collected by the ocean and how many living organisms are affected by it.

My professional responsibilities onboard the ship granted me the unique opportunity to daily witness life out at sea. The reoccurring theme of beauty, complexity, and awe became an integral part of my experiences as a watch and helmsman onboard the ship. My experiences ranged from witnessing the clear and calm blue waters of the Mediterranean and Caribbean Sea to the stormy and freezing waters of the Atlantic Ocean.

After my naval career, I lived in Virginia Beach, Virginia, for a year. I was disturbed by the commercial industries that lined the beach. These industries attracted visitors from all over the world. The need for environmental stewardship became self-evident when I saw the amount of trash and waste left behind after major events that were held there. However, I did not discover the real impact of consumerism on the environment until I learned about the power of consumer choices. This is when I realized the linkage between consumer choices and environmental toxins released in communities located next to fossil fuel, chemical, and manufacturing plants locally and globally. At that moment, I became overwhelmed by my moral responsibility to care for the poor. I joined the climate justice movement to work with the poor to end the unprecedented impacts of pollution and natural disasters on vulnerable communities throughout the world.

Climate justice mobilizes citizens, scientists, activists, and the poor to challenge policymakers and corporations to invest in clean energy and eliminate waste. We are now aware that global warming causes severe thunderstorms, hurricanes, flooding, droughts, and record-breaking temperatures. Today, human consumption is directly connected to the rise of global temperatures because of our dependency on fossil fuels and deforestation. We depend on oil, coal, and natural gas for energy to heat and cool our homes, light our communities, and provide fuel for transportation. We depend on deforestation to grow food, dispose of waste, build new homes, and expand economic development. Fossil fuels and deforestation make up 74 percent of the global greenhouse gas emissions.[1] Climate justice focuses on transforming every person into a steward of the earth's resources. According to the Genesis accounts of creation, humans are created in the image of God and serve as God's caretakers of creation. These stories of creation show us God's perspective on the sacred trust given to humans to care for what God created, saw, and said was very good—capable of sustaining life (Genesis 1–3).

In the beginning, the world had an abundant supply of pure water to drink, clean air to breathe, nutritious food to eat, and expansive forests to sustain human life. God created pure water, available in the groundwater, springs, creeks, rivers, and marshes, to quench our thirst. God made nutritional food, available through a diversity of fish, plants, and wildlife that live in water, forests, plains, and marshes, to satisfy our hunger. God created oxygen, by causing the trees to inhale carbon dioxide and exhale oxygen, to give us the breath of life. God created a climate to regulate the rising and falling of global temperatures, to regulate the seasons of life, and to sustain life on earth. Then, God saw everything that God created and said it was very good.

Through the eyes of God, Adam and Eve were aware of how everything in nature is connected by design and dependent on God as the source of life. Adam and Eve listened to every species of plants, trees, fish, marine organisms, birds, and wildlife and learned how everything reproduces its own kind. They listened to the voice of God teaching them how to care for the needs of every living organism in Eden. They lived in an oasis and maintained the sacred balance between what was taken from the earth and what was returned to the earth. They ate from the Tree of Life and kept the sacred trust given to humanity to act as the presence of God in human form, caring for each other and nature. The Tree of Life gave Adam and Eve a vision of the world that was limitless. Their choices and actions could not be distinguished from God's choices and actions in the world. Humanity was able to see how they were connected to God, each other, and nature. The story of creation ends with Adam and Eve eating from the Tree of Knowledge of Good and Evil and breaking the covenant they had with God.

> Now the serpent was more crafty than any other wild animal that God had [created]. He said to [Eve], "Did God say, 'You shall not eat from any tree in the garden'?" [Eve] said to the serpent, "We may eat of the fruit of the trees in the garden; but God said, 'You shall not eat of the fruit of the tree that is in the middle of the garden, nor shall you touch it, or you shall die.'" But the serpent said to [Eve], "You will not die; for God knows that when you eat of it your eyes will be opened, and you will be like God, knowing good and evil." So when the woman saw that the tree was good for food, and that it was a delight to the eyes, and the tree was to be desired to make one wise, she took of its fruit and ate; and she also gave to her husband, who was with her, and he ate. Then the eyes of

both were opened [to knowing good and evil], and they knew that they were naked; and they sewed fig leaves together and made loincloths for themselves. (Genesis 3:1–7)

The Tree of the Knowledge of Good and Evil gave humanity a vision of the world that was limited because Adam and Eve no longer saw themselves and nature from God's vantage point. This is when sin entered the world and humans no longer sought God's wisdom to guide their choices and actions. Before Adam and Eve sinned, they asked God for wisdom before taking from nature to satisfy their biological needs and desires. After Adam and Eve sinned, humanity depended on the limitations of human wisdom to find water, grow food, and satisfy their desires. God responded to the unwise choices of humans by establishing covenants with Noah, Abraham, David, and Moses to teach humanity how to love each other and care for nature. In each generation, prophets were sent to show us how to restore our broken covenants with God by not trusting "the desire of the flesh, the desire of the eyes, the pride in riches" (1 John 2:16), but in the wisdom of God.

Christ was sent into the world to become the Second Adam and establish a new covenant with humanity by expanding our concept of neighbor (Luke 10:25–37). This new concept of loving your neighbor included everyone in the world in spite of his or her social or economic status (John 3:16; Galatians 3:15–29). Jesus' ministry defied the cultural logic of his community by commanding that the love we show ourselves is equal to the love we show our neighbor (Mark 12:31). The climate justice movement spreads the gospel message by advocating that the love we show ourselves in the wealthiest countries is equal to the love we show others in the poorest countries. Christians from wealthy and poor countries are uniting to create ministries with the poor to give everyone equal access to pure

water, clean air, nutritious food, healthy homes, and safe communities regardless of their social or economic status.

The Gospel According to Climate Justice

From the point of view of the author of the book of John, Christ was present when God taught Adam and Eve to nurture every plant, tree, fish, marine organism, bird, and animal to grow and reproduce their own kind. Christ was also present when God showed humanity how to cultivate loving relationships and watched each generation break their covenant with God and each other (John 1:1–18). For Christ, the only way to heal creation and humanity from the unwise decisions of each generation was to produce a new generation of followers that practiced the ministry of reconciliation.

> From now on, therefore, we regard no one from a human point of view, even though we once knew Christ from a human point of view, we see him no longer in that way. So if anyone is in Christ, there is a new creation: everything old has passed away; see, everything has become new! All this is from God, who reconciled us to himself through Christ, and has given us the ministry of reconciliation; that is, in Christ God was reconciling the world to himself, not counting their trespasses against them, and entrusting the message of reconciliation to us. So we are ambassadors for Christ, since God is making his appeal through us; we entreat you on behalf of Christ, be reconciled to God. For our sake he made him to be sin who knew no sin, so that in him we might become the righteousness of God. (2 Corinthians 5:16–21)

Christ's message of reconciliation is spread throughout the world using parables that connect spiritual growth to environmental stewardship. For example, in the parable of the sower and the seeds and the parable of the weeds, Christ opens the disciples' eyes to show them how the message of reconciliation will be spread throughout the world. The sower in both parables mirrors how Jesus sows the seeds of reconciliation in communities. The disciples learned how to grow Christian communities by connecting the environmental factors needed to produce natural food to the environmental factors needed to produce spiritual food. The parable of the sower and the seeds illustrates how the condition of a person's heart (hard, stony, rocky, or good) determines how he or she will respond to the seeds of reconciliation. In the same way, the condition of the soil (hard, stony, rocky, or good) determines how the soil will respond to seeds from a sower (Matthew 13:1–23). In the parable of the weeds, the disciples' knowledge of agriculture and crop management gave them the ability to see each other as seeds of reconciliation (seeds of wheat) being sown in the community by the hands of God. The disciples were also able to envision how seeds of dissension (seeds of weed) will be sown in the same community by the hands of the evil one. These allegories[2] teach us that Jesus will sow his disciples as good seeds to unite communities while the evil one will sow followers as evil seeds to divide communities (Matthew 13:24–30; 36–43).

The gospel according to climate justice teaches us how to produce the fruits of the Spirit in communities overwhelmed by the weeds of climate change—unpredictable weather patterns, rising sea levels, deforestation increasing pests, decline in fisheries, destruction of ecosystems, and the extinction of species. Christians joining the climate justice movement spread the good news that God's love for wealthy communities is equal to God's love for poor and vulnerable communities. In turn, Christians produce the fruits of "love, joy, peace, patience, kindness, generosity, faithfulness, gentleness, and self-control" (Galatians 5:22–23) in barren communities to sustain life. Christians are also responding to the fruits of hate with love, misery with joy, impatience with

patience, brutality with kindness, selfishness with generosity, disloyalty with faithfulness, callousness with gentleness, and greed with self-control to unite communities divided over climate change. From a religious point of view, Christians are able to discern whether a person's heart is hard, stony, thorny, or good ground and how working with each person can remove the social and economic barriers to climate justice. Christians are equally called to work on energy, water, and habitat conservation projects; create policies that reduce greenhouse gas emissions and pollution; as well as unite communities divided over climate justice. We work with the poor toward guaranteeing that the most vulnerable communities have access to pure water, clean air, nutritious food, healthy homes, and safe communities that is equal to the access wealthy people in developed and developing countries enjoy.

As Christians, we have been given the challenge to reduce our carbon emissions to zero in our lifetimes. The future of humanity and creation are linked in God's message of universal salvation. To save humanity is to save creation; to save creation is to save humanity (Romans 8:18–25). God designed the plan of salvation to ensure that we return to our original purpose and recreate Eden on earth. In the parable of the sheep and the goats, Christ further illustrates how we will be judged in the end by how we cared for the most vulnerable in our community and world. The truest indicator of success by Jesus' disciples was whether or not they saw all other persons as they see Christ. This way of seeing each other does not allow for Christians to discriminate based on a person's social or economic status in society. Everyone is equal in Christ's eyes and we will not be judged based on how well we treat those with the most wealth but how well we treat those with the fewest resources.

Then the king [Christ] will say to those at his right hand, "Come, you that are blessed by my Father, inherit the kingdom prepared for you from the foundation of the world; for I was hungry and you gave me food, I was thirsty and you gave me something to drink, I was a stranger and you welcomed me, I was naked and you gave me clothing, I was sick and you took care of me, I was in prison and you visited me." Then the righteous will answer him, "Lord, when was it that we saw you hungry and gave you food, or thirsty and gave you something to drink? And when was it that we saw you a stranger and welcomed you, or naked and gave you clothing? And when was it that we saw you sick or in prison and visited you?" And the king will answer them, "Truly I tell you, just as you did it to one of the least of these who are members of my family, you did it to me." (Matthew 25:34–40)

In the climate justice movement, the Christian commitment to all people who are impacted by climate change is not separate from our commitment to Christ. The seeds of climate change were planted when human communities sought their own wisdom instead of God's wisdom to care for each other and nature. When Christians serve the poor and most vulnerable as a result of severe thunderstorms, hurricanes, flooding, droughts and record-breaking temperatures, we are planting seeds of climate justice (Matthew 25:31–46). This parable reminds us that Christians are those on the right hand of Christ who became seeds of reconciliation and connected their vision of personal holiness to social holiness. As we minister with the poor and become environmental stewards, we remain faithful to God's vision of salvation for the world promised through Jesus Christ.

Climate Change and the Pursuit of Happiness

The United States has just 5 percent of the world's population, but is the second largest contributor of the world's carbon dioxide emissions after China.[3] Climate change is caused by national and global economies that are dependent on fossil fuels and consume it in unsustainable quantities. The result is that disadvantaged nations and populations, particularly women, that contribute the least to the causes of climate change suffer the most negative consequences from it.

United Methodist Women acknowledges the connection between the overdependence on fossil fuels from developing countries and its effect on the poor, women, and children who bear the unjust burden of starvation, disease, sickness, unemployment, and death because of global warming. The increased demand for fossil fuels in the United States is intricately connected to each American's pursuit of happiness (including water, food, land, health, job, property, and personal security). America has historically secured its pursuit of happiness by working with citizens, policymakers, and corporations to build a national and global economy that supports consumerism.

Today, this economic model has proven to be unsustainable because of the limited access to fossil fuels and the high cost of protecting Americans from the devastating effects of unpredictable fires, droughts, floods, hurricanes, and tornadoes. Christians are uniquely poised to enter the climate justice movement and infuse a faith-based approach to climate change that will ensure that the poor, women, and children are not repeatedly crushed by the weight of environmental toxins and disasters.

To illuminate the direct link between the pursuit of happiness in developed countries and the unhappiness it creates in disadvantaged communities, I would like to share the Happiness Machine story:

> Once upon a time there was a kingdom of people who pursued happiness. Nothing was more important to them than being happy. The happier they became, the happier they wanted to be. The source of the people's happiness was a magic Happiness Machine.

Whenever the people felt unhappy they would pour their troubled feelings into the Happiness Machine. The magic machine would melt their feelings down and purify them. The residue of their troubles became dross, and the dross was drained away and dumped into a distant part of the kingdom. The people would take their purified feelings and go away singing and feeling happy again. They were called the "Happy People."

As the years and centuries went by, the Happy People became happier and happier because of the wonderful effects of the Happiness Machine. There was only one problem. Another group of people lived in a distant part of the kingdom where all the dross was dumped. The dross made them very unhappy.

They were called the "Unhappy People." The more dross that was dumped on them, the unhappier they became. However, the Unhappy People were not permitted to use the Happiness Machine, because the one thing the magic machine could not do was purify its own dross.

The Unhappy People complained to the Happy People about the problems they had with the dross. But the Happy People ignored their complaints. When they were confronted with the troubling results of their happiness, the Happy People simply took their troubled feelings to the Happiness Machine, and it made them happy again. It was easy to believe that it was not the dross of their own troubles that made other people unhappy. Rather, they convinced themselves that the Unhappy People were just incurably unhappy and that they had nobody but themselves to blame for their unhappiness.

It was not long before the Unhappy People began to protest more insistently about their situation. They organized marches and demonstrations. They demanded that the dross be removed from their part of the kingdom. And they demanded a fair share of happiness for their people. But the Happy People turned a deaf ear to their protests, which only served to make the Unhappy People unhappier, and they protested all the more.

Finally, the Happy People could no longer ignore the protests. They used force to put down the protesters, and arrested and jailed the leaders. They passed laws and organized military force to control the Unhappy People. Many of the Unhappy People were killed. This only made them unhappier. They began to plot and plan how they could destroy the Happiness Machine.

The conflict and tension caused a severe drain on the Happy People's happiness.

To make it worse, some of the Happy People were becoming increasingly troubled about the way the Unhappy People were being treated. All these new troubles made the Happiness Machine work even harder, and as a result even more dross was produced. They had to build an even bigger and better Happiness Machine to take care of the happiness needs of the Happy People. Consequently, the dross was piled higher and higher and spread farther and farther into other parts of the kingdom, which made more and more Unhappy People. It was not long before the Unhappy People were in a constant state of rebellion.

Then a new and even greater danger arose. The Happiness Machine had become so large and productive that there was no place left in the kingdom to put the dross. The piles of dross crept closer and closer to the homes of the Happy People and to the place where the Happiness Machine was operating. There was an ominous threat that the dross would back up into its own machine, and the machine would self-destruct. Now the Happy People were troubled not only by the rebellion of the Unhappy People, but also by their own Happiness Machine.

The new danger caused even greater internal troubles among the Happy People. Some people began to sorrowfully predict that the Happiness Machine would soon self-destruct. Others suggested that the only alternative was to build an even bigger Happiness Machine in order to deal with the crisis they were facing. Others began to see that the Happiness Machine was not the solution to their problems, but the cause. They wanted to reduce the size of the Happiness Machine, or even dismantle it altogether. Some even began to wish that they could join together with the Unhappy People and build a new society together without the help of Happiness Machines.

The end of this story has not yet been written.[4]

This story is an invitation to the reader to see themselves as part of the story and to help write its ending. To illustrate the connection between climate justice and creation care, I offer a different ending to the Happiness Machine story based on the United States' pursuit of happiness:

The *Happiness Machine* mirrors the emergence of the climate justice movement. The increased demand for pure water, nutritional foods, jobs, health care, commercial buildings, and private property in the United States has contributed to climate change. The prosperity of our country relies heavily on being able to extract, produce, and import natural resources from developing countries to maintain our way of life. The source of happiness for many Americans is pouring their feelings into the Happiness Machine and consuming more products to maintain their happiness. The dross (carbon dioxide and toxic waste) increases as more American consumers seek consumption as the only solution to their crisis of feeling unhappy. When Americans realized that there was not enough land to store the dross in poor communities of America, they began dumping the dross in developing countries. The poor in the United States and in developing countries began to complain to policymakers and resist corporations dumping toxic waste in their backyards. However, their complaints were ignored and hope for climate justice was deferred by corporations finding alternative sources for oil, coal, natural gas, chemicals, and manufactured goods to keep up with the demand for more happiness.

…As the years and centuries went by, the Happy People [privileged Americans] became happier and happier because of the wonderful effects of the Happiness Machine [consumerism]. There was only one problem. Another group of people lived in a distant part of [the United States and developing countries] where all the dross was dumped. The dross made them very unhappy.

They were called the "Unhappy People" [the poor and most vulnerable people to climate change]. The more dross that was dumped on them, the unhappier they became. [The Unhappy People experience record-breaking heat, rainfall, snow, drought, and multi-million dollar losses from extreme flooding.] However, the Unhappy People were [only given access to toxic water, air, land and poisoned food], because the one thing the magic machine could not do was purify its own dross. The Unhappy People complained to the Happy People about the problems they had with the dross.

[And some Happy People joined the Climate Justice Movement after hearing the Unhappy People's complaints. The Happy People began to examine how much they depended on the Happiness Machine to make them happy. The Happy People questioned how their overdependence on fossil fuels produced inequality in poor communities and developing countries. Rather than blame the Unhappy People for their unhappiness, the Happy People began to blame the Happiness Machine they had created.]

It was not long before [Christians in the Climate Justice Movement] began to protest more insistently about [the Unhappy People's] situation [to the other Happy People]. They organized community meetings and joined marches and demonstrations. They became lobbyists and advocates to sow seeds of reconciliation in communities divided over climate change. They demanded that the dross be removed from [the Unhappy People's communities]. And they demanded a fair share of happiness for [ALL] people. [The other] Happy People [listened] to their protests, which [made] the Unhappy People [happier], and they [sat down with the Happy People to learn how to listen to the wisdom of God, each other, and creation as they began to change policies and laws to reduce, reuse, and recycle the dross].

Finally, the Happy People [released the leaders of the Climate Justice Movement who were arrested, jailed, and imprisoned. They changed the laws and ended the use of military force to control the Unhappy People]. The Happy People changed their plans to build an even bigger and better Happiness Machine [based on fossil fuels] to take care of the happiness needs of the Happy People. The Happy People designed new plans to dismantle the Happiness Machine [and create alternative sources for clean and renewable energy that produced zero dross]. All rebellions ceased and [everyone] began to build a new society based on environmental stewardship.[5]

This story is one among many of how people of faith can teach God's love for humanity and creation. The ending of this story has not been written and I only offer insights into what may be possible if we look at global warming and our participation in the climate justice movement from the vantage point of God. ✪

Endnotes

1. "Global Greenhouse Gas Emissions Data," The United States Environmental Protection Agency, accessed May 18, 2015, www.epa.gov/climatechange/ghgemissions/global.html.

2. Other allegories that illustrate how Jesus connects spiritual growth to environmental stewardship based on the disciples' understanding of marine biology, mammalogy, and agriculture are the parables of new wine in old wineskins (Luke 5:37–38); the barren fig tree (Luke 13:6–9); the mustard seed (Mark 4:30–32); the yeast (Luke 13:20–21); the fishing net (Matthew 13:47–50); and the budding fig tree (Matthew 24:32–35).

3. "CO2 time series 1990-2013 per region/country," Emission Database for Global Atmospheric Research, accessed October 19, 2015, http://edgar.jrc.ec.europa.eu/overview.php.

4. Joseph Barndt, *Understanding and Dismantling Racism: The Twenty-First Century Challenge to White America* (New York: Fortress Press, 2007), 1–3.

5. Ibid.

About the Author

I. Malik Saafir is the cofounder and president of Janus Institute For Justice, a nonprofit organization based in Central Arkansas committed to environmental and social justice. Saafir has devoted his career to the study of the intersection between religion, ethics, and culture, seeking to end racial, economic, and health disparities in low-income communities.

Saafir also trains advocates and activists on how to interpret, translate, and apply theories of justice through social and environmental justice projects. He holds a master's degree in adult education (M. Ed.) from the University of Arkansas at Little Rock (UALR) and a master's of divinity (M. Div.) from Vanderbilt University where he was a Kelly Miller Smith Scholar and graduated with honors.

Saafir currently serves on the board of directors for Arkansas Interfaith Power and Light and Green-Faith—two nonprofit organizations for environmental justice. He also serves on the UALR Institute for Race and Ethnicity Steering Committee. His most recent accomplishment is becoming a GreenFaith Fellow and Toyota Together Green Fellow.

Cesar Chavez High School in Houston, Texas. *Photo by Juan Parras*

Chapter 4

Climate Injustice: How Did We Get Here?

Jacqueline Patterson

WHETHER IT'S A CHART-TOPPING hip-hop song titled "It's All About the Benjamins" or 2012 presidential candidate Mitt Romney referring to a group of millionaires as "my base," or the fact that the average coal company CEO earns 289 times as much as the company's workers, the signs that wealth is a major value in Western culture abound. However, due to the way "the rules" are written, the wealth is heavily concentrated among the rule makers. For eample, just one percent of the U.S. population has 35.6 percent of all private wealth, worth more than the wealth of all of the people in the bottom 95 percent combined.[1]

We find ourselves in an unfettered slide toward catastrophic climate change, a predicament that is rooted in our commoditization of labor and natural resources that amasses wealth for a powerful few. Colonization had the central aim of acquiring natural resources (spices, minerals, gold, etc.), land, and people.

It is a well-known fact that when Christopher Columbus set off he considered himself to be "ordained by God" and that his mission was purported to be two-fold: to spread the gospel and advance material conquest. As this group of voyagers encountered indigenous people along the way, the conquest goal expanded to include the acquisition of free labor in addition to land and natural resources. In fact, nonacceptance of the gospel was a church-approved rationale for enslavement and even war. "When encountering a people, the requerimiento was to read to them. Afterwards, if they still chose not to submit to God's will, violence was permissible."[2] Using their non-Christianity as the foundation, the dehumanization of people into vessels of slave labor was fully permissible by the church. "Indians had to be Christian before they could even be considered human."[3]

The industrialization period of rapid economic growth and soaring prosperity in the Northern and Western hemispheres, saw the United States become the world's dominant economic, industrial, and agricultural power. Accompanying this advancement was the promise of a better life for all, with an underlying message that riches can be gained by anyone who works hard enough and perseveres. However, this vision didn't match the reality as the industrial period perpetuated the same patterns in a new context. The growth of the Western world was accompanied by an explosion of land acquisition and natural resources with continued reliance on cheap labor. Wages surged for some and remained stagnant for others, especially for the farmers upon whose backs agricultural power was amassed. The system continued to stack the deck for a privileged few, while oppressing others and violating the rights of people of color, and indigenous people in particular.

With few notable exceptions, the church has failed to make a shift to recognize the systemic change that is needed to improve the lives of "the least of these" it purports to serve. On one hand, we have a proliferation of megachurches and others preaching the "prosperity gospel," which perpetuates values of the acquisition of wealth and lifestyles of excess. Whether it's communities of color and low-income communities in the United States or countries in the Global South, the emphasis is on encouraging folks to engage with the church (and give to the church) with a view toward saving souls and helping folks move toward the utopian concept of sharing the riches of Western culture. On the other hand we have, albeit well-meaning, churches that see their role as limited to providing social services and caring for the poor through handouts, which is certainly critical; however most fall short of taking up the mantle of examining structural inequality and advocating for the transformative shifts that are necessary to eliminate poverty.

A key loss that has befallen the church in its misplaced focus on wealth has been the fulfillment of its critical role as steward of God's creation. John Wesley's teachings tell us "money should be regarded as a gift of God for the benefits that it brings in ordering the affairs of civilization and the opportunities it offers for doing good."[4] In this, Wesley denounces waste and luxury and emphasizes responsible stewardship for the well-being of all people. However, in its distraction with wealth for the sake of excess, the church has disconnected itself from a relationship with God's creation. Instead of valuing the land as God's original design intended to sustain us, the church has bought into the idea that the land is a resource to be heedlessly exploited, and in so doing has abdicated its role as protector.

As we moved into the age of globalization, we started to see new ways of furthering structural inequality by exporting jobs to avoid labor laws that call for fair wages. These new systems also perpetuated the extraction of natural resources with little regard for the impact within our shores and overseas where we were able to avoid environmental regulations.

While the church too often sleeps at the switch, the methods of the ruling classes (brute force and extraction) and the mono-focus on building wealth with no concern for human rights or the well-being of the earth persists even today. We no longer call these actions "colonization," but "development." Development, as defined by Western culture is rooted in capitalism, which means there must be winners and losers. For example, rules were made that locked out certain countries from manufacturing while they were exploited for their natural resources. One article on the topic notes that for more than 82 years Firestone "has run the world's largest rubber operation in the world in a financially exploitative relationship using child labor to extract rubber from Liberia without paying proper taxes" to the government.[5] The development construct and its accompanying rules imposed by the World Bank, the International Monetary Fund, the World Trade Organization, and various entities in the U.S. federal, state, and local governments have institutionalized systems whereby countries in the Global South and communities of color and low-income communities in the United States disproportionately suffer from development processes while they have little voice in decision making.

Most relevant to the issue of climate change are the subsidization of the fossil fuel industry and the lack of regulations governing its practices, which are destroying the environment and violating human rights. Fossil fuel companies reap $550 billion per year in subsidies. On average, oil, coal, and gas received more than four times the $120 billion paid out in incentives for renewables including wind and solar.[6]

Entities, such as the American Legislative Exchange Council (ALEC) and the Americans for Prosperity (Koch Brothers), that are most invested in the fossil fuel industry spend millions of dollars annually to influence research produced by academic institutions and think tanks, as well as who holds elected offices and the courts and the decisions they make. These decisions are directly related to the energy industry, including blocking regulations protecting air, water, and land, and legislation on energy efficiency and clean energy, as well as furthering the disenfranchisement of those who would advance systems changes, such as low-income communities and communities of color. The Koch brothers alone spent $61 million dollars between 1997 and 2010 to support climate-denying institutions that lobby against clean air and clean energy legislation.[7]

As a result, we have a trillion-dollar energy economy that is built on the tenets of concentrated wealth, total disregard for environmental impact, and depression of wages and workers' rights.

- Subsurface coal mining has taken place on indigenous lands, in many cases defiling sacred ground. At the same time, the mining industry has spent millions of dollars over the years in antiregulatory lobbying against measures that can protect workers' health. As a result, since 1968, 76,000 coal miners died of black lung disease until the first-ever regulation on coal dust went into effect on August 1, 2014.[8]
- Coal combustion is not only the top emitter of carbon dioxide, but it also impacts the health and well-being of communities that are host to coal plants due to the emission of co-pollutants including mercury, arsenic, lead, sulfur dioxide, nitrogen oxide, and more! These toxins are tied to respiratory illnesses, birth defects, attention-deficit disorder, and even learning problems. Close proximity to toxic facilities causes

property-value depreciation of 15 percent on average.[9] All of these impacts are disproportionately borne by communities of color and low-income communities, as these neighborhoods are most likely to be hosts to coal-fired power plants.
- Mountaintop-removal mining to extract the coal within has contaminated our waterways destroying whole species of fish,[10] damaged home foundations, compromised health outcomes, and defiled once beautiful vistas.
- Extraction and refining of oil has resulted in catastrophic spills and drilling disasters such as the Exxon Valdez and the BP oil spills, which caused loss of life, property, waterways, livelihoods, and culture. In Thibodaux, Louisiana, land is actually sinking due to the excessive drilling that happens off its coast. Between the sinking land and the rising sea level, coastal Louisiana is losing an average of a football field of land every hour.[11] As a result, residents of Thibodaux will have to move within twenty years.
- In addition to extraction and combustion processes, another hazard is transporting fossil fuels, which is at the center of the controversy around the Keystone XL oil pipeline and various crude-by-rail projects. Between incidents such as the train explosion in Quebec that literally disintegrated parts of a town to the extent that bodies were never found,[12] and the pipeline explosion in New Mexico that killed ten campers,[13] the evidence of the danger in moving oil and gas is clear.

Even as advocacy by environmental and human rights groups resulting in increased regulations has advanced a shift in the industry and the market, the alternatives being pursued are often just as harmful as the traditional energy production processes.

- The incentives to advance ethanol as a gasoline alternative by growing corn for fuel have resulted in the clear-cutting of precious rainforests.
- Public pressure that has shut down coal plants and increased regulations, has led the industry to seek cheaper alternatives, particularly natural gas. Unfortunately, the hydraulic fracturing used to extract natural gas emits significant levels of methane, has been linked to an increase in seismic activities (earthquakes), and has resulted in heightened explosivity levels in the water supplies of people near fracking sites, among other problems.[14]
- Nuclear energy, another energy source, even cited in the "Clean Power Plan,"[15] is troubling from cradle to grave. The challenges of uranium mining are well acknowledged. In Kayenta, Arizona, one place in the United States where uranium is mined, there is a dedicated health clinic for uranium mineworkers. There are documented cancer clusters near mining sites or reactors.[16] And the disaster at Fukushima Daiichi in Japan is a cautionary tale given the proliferation of nuclear reactors located in earthquake fault zones in the United States.

- Clean coal or carbon capture and sequestration is an extremely expensive and not yet fully proven technology for lowering carbon emissions from the combustion of coal. However, even if this process were successful in containing carbon, it doesn't take care of co-pollutants nor does it resolve extraction issues or safe disposal of coal ash, which are persistent concerns.

Because we have been on this path of harmful extraction practices and extreme excesses in both the use and wasting of energy for decades, the United States is responsible for over 39 percent of cumulative carbon emissions though it has only 4 percent of the world's population.[17] At the same time, the United States is most resistant to change, as it was one of the only nations that did not sign onto the Kyoto Protocol, an international treaty that committed State Parties to reduce greenhouse gas emissions, and continues to advance low ambition in the climate talks of the annual UN Framework Convention on Climate Change (UNFCCC) Conference of Parties (COP).

In the lead-up to the 2014 UNFCCC COP 20, the United States forged an agreement with China, as the two top polluters, to pledge to

United Methodist Women members participated in the People's Climate March, New York City, September 2014. *Photo by Pat Watkins*

reduce emissions. President Obama is setting a new target for the United States, agreeing to cut greenhouse gas emissions to 26 to 28 percent below 2005 levels by 2025. The current U.S. target is to reach a level of 17 percent below 2005 emissions by 2020. China agreed to reduce its emissions by leveling out its rising levels by 2030 or before, and to increase its non-fossil fuel share of energy production to about 20 percent by 2030.[18] They also agreed on joint research, trade on green technology/products, piloting clean energy products, etc. The United States then committed $3 billion to the Green Climate Fund.[19]

There is growing recognition that the planet cannot sustain this unfettered excess. Sadly, one reason for this is that the resources we are irresponsibly extracting and burning, resulting in these harmful emissions, are finite. At the same time, 97 percent of climate scientists agree that the world is warming as a result of human action. Scientific evidence, coupled with the major disasters we are seeing (wide-scale droughts, wildfires, and megastorms like Katrina, Sandy, and Haiyan), has led the world to take notice and feel increasingly compelled to change.

With converging climate and economic crises, as well as the increasing number of conflicts around the world, a growing number of people have begun to recognize that our systems are broken. We saw the popularity of the Occupy Movement, the significant turnout for the People's Climate March, etc., as signs that people are acknowledging the need for systemic change and calling for reform. There is a concentrated movement to move resources and power from monopolies around energy, agriculture, waste, etc. People and neighborhoods are advancing models for strengthening local economies through collective/cooperative organizing. We are seeing the proliferation of community-owned solar and recycling programs. Community groups are reconnecting with the land and implementing local food projects.

As we make these shifts on the individual and community levels, there are also larger conversations at regional, national, and global levels. Advocates are pushing for policies that support decentralization and structural measures to operationalize a true democracy. At the UNFCCC, there are some critical questions being asked about who bears the most responsibility for climate change and what it means for developing economies such as China, India, and Brazil. These nations are emerging powers that are actively engaging in industrialization and globalization simultaneously. However, what will be the environmental consequences of that development? Already, China has surpassed the United States as the nation responsible for the largest proportion of global emissions. But the question is, as these nations grow, do we have the right to demand lifestyles and regulations that we have not implemented ourselves? There is a similar tension in U.S. communities, such as some communities of color and low-income communities. Some of them have struggled for decades to achieve the "American dream," which is defined by some level of acquisition of wealth/status. Now the target is shifting as we engage in the systemic change we need to uplift rights for all people. In some ways we need to work on redefining the dream by measuring not just economic equity but *buen vivir* or the "good life" with indicators around happiness, fulfillment, well-being, etc.

Where we've come from and how we've arrived at this juncture of climate injustice can be chronicled through the evolution of our socio-economic and political landscape as well as a collection of oral histories of lived experiences. To see real transformation, our challenge is to address the root causes of the climate crisis, including structural inequality, lack of real democracy, and the myopic pursuit of wealth through the commoditization of labor and natural resources. ✪

Endnotes

1. "Facts and Figures in 99 to 1," Inequality.org, accessed May 18, 2015, http://inequality.org/99to1/facts-figures/#sthash.RU7xQLTs.dpuf.

2. Miguel Leon-Portilla, *The Broken Spears: The Aztec Account of the Conquest of Mexico* (Boston: Beacon Press, 1992).

3. Hernando Cortes, *Five Letters of Cortes to the Emperor: 1519–1526* (New York: W.W. Norton & Company, 1991).

4. John Wesley, Sermon 44, "Original Sin," *The Sermons of John Wesley*, General Board of Global Ministries of The United Methodist Church, www.umcmission.org/Find-Resources/John-Wesley-Sermons/Sermon-44-Original-Sin.

5. Ashahed Muhammad, "The Exploitation of Africa's Land and People," *The Final Call*, February 24, 2009, www.finalcall.com/artman/publish/World_News_3/The_exploitation_of_Africa_s_land_and_people_5661.shtml.

6. Alex Morales, "Fossil Fuels with $550 Billion Subsidies Hurt Renewables," Bloomberg Business, November 12, 2014, www.bloomberg.com/news/2014-11-12/fossil-fuels-with-550-billion-in-subsidy-hurt-renewables.html.

7. Connor Gibson, "Koch Brothers Exposed: Fueling Climate Denial and Privatizing Democracy," Greenpeace blog, updated June 20, 2012, http://greenpeaceblogs.org/2012/04/02/koch-brothers-exposed-fueling-climate-denial-and-privatizing-democracy.

8. "First Phase of MSHA's Respirable Coal Mine Dust Rule Goes into Effect," United States Department of Labor, July 31, 2014, www.dol.gov/opa/media/press/msha/MSHA20141426.htm.

9. A.K. Reichert, "Impact of a Toxic Superfund Site on Property Value," *The Appraisal Journal* 65 (October 1997): 381–392.

10. Matt Wasson, "Study Shows Steep Decline in Fish Population Near Mountain Top Removal," Appalachian Voices, August 10, 2014, http://appvoices.org/2014/08/10/study-shows-steep-decline-in-fish-populations-near-mountaintop-removal.

11. "How are Louisiana Wetlands Changing?" United States Geological Survey, June 2, 2011, www.usgs.gov/newsroom/article_pf.asp?ID=2816.

12. "Lac-Megantic Train Explosion: Three Charged in Quebec," BBC News, May 13, 2014, www.bbc.com/news/world-us-canada-27387287.

13. "Pipeline Explosion Kills 10 Campers in N.M.," ABC News, August 20, 2000, http://abcnews.go.com/US/story?id=96090.

14. Pietje Vervest, Timothé Feodoroff, et al., "No Fracking Way," March 6, 2014, TNI Environmental Justice, www.tni.org/briefing/no-fracking-way.

15. "Clean Power Plan Proposed Rule," Environmental Protection Agency, June 2, 2014, www2.epa.gov/carbon-pollution-standards/clean-power-plan-proposed-rule.

16. Regina Medina, "US: Report Finds High Rate of Thyroid Cancer in Eastern Pennsylvania; Blames Nuclear Power Plants," sott. net, January 22, 2010, www.sott.net/article/ 201699-US-Report-finds-high-rate-of-thyroid-cancer-in-eastern-Pennsylvania-blames-nuclear-power-plants, and Brent Hunsaker, "Uranium Mill Blamed for Cancer Cluster in Monticello," Disease Cluster Communities, Utah, May 6, 2010, http:// clusteralliance.org/2010/05/06/uranium-mill-blamed-for-cancer-cluster-in-monticello.

17. "Who is Most Responsible for Climate Change?" The Energy Collective, September 30, 2013, http://theenergycollective.com/ ivonnepena/281366/who-most-responsible-climate-change-infographic.

18. Phil Mattingly and David J. Lynch, "U.S., China Agree to New Cuts to Combat Climate Change," Bloomberg Politics, November 11, 2014, www.bloomberg.com/ news/2014-11-12/u-s-china-agree-to-new-cuts-to-combat-climate-change.html.

19. Coral Davenport and Mark Landler, "U.S. to Give $3 Billion to Climate Fund to Help Poor Nations, and Spur Rich Ones," *The New York Times*, November 14, 2014, www. nytimes.com/2014/11/15/us/politics/ obama-climate-change-fund-3-billion-announcement.html?_r=0.

End Boulevard Interchange and the surrounding area of northwest New Orleans and Metairie, Louisiana, after Hurricane Katrina. *Photo by Mfield*

About the Author

Jacqueline Patterson (Jacqui) is the director of the National Association for the Advancement of Colored People (NAACP) Climate Gap Initiative. She was born and raised on the south side of Chicago to a Jamaican immigrant father and an African-American mother from Mississippi. She attended Boston University where she earned a bachelor's degree in special education while working in the Boston shelter system and participating in the Housing Now movement. During her three-and-a-half-year term as a volunteer with the U.S. Peace Corps in Jamaica, Patterson worked with the Community Environmental Resource Center, which began due to the contamination of the Harbour View community water supply by the neighboring Shell Company plant. After the Peace Corps, Patterson went on to earn two master's degrees in public health and social work from Johns Hopkins University and the University of Maryland respectively.

Patterson has worked as a trainer, organizer, researcher, program manager, and policy analyst on international and domestic issues and social justice movements with organizations including Center on Budget and Policy Priorities, Baltimore City Healthy Start, IMA World Health, United for a Fair Economy, ActionAid, Health GAP, and the organization she co-founded, Women of Color United (WOCU). Patterson is now the Climate Justice Initiative Director for the NAACP. Her work on climate justice before engaging with the NAACP was through Women of Color United's participation in a Movement Generation for Change Ecology Justice Retreat and partnership with the Women's Environment and Development Organization on the From Katrina to Copenhagen Initiative. Last year, she facilitated a partnership between the NAACP and Women of Color United to engage in the Women of Color for Climate Justice Road Tour to uplift stories of differential impact, local community self-reliance, and community resistance of women of color and communities of color.

The abuse of the earth by humans has consequences for all of God's creation.
Photo by Manfred Thürig

Chapter 5

Climate Injustice: Earth Consequences

Dottie Yunger

Our Island Home and Rules to Live By

In 2003, while working for the Smithsonian Institution as a marine biologist and environmental educator, I spent two weeks on a small island off the coast of Belize with a group of American college students. Calabash Caye is in the Belize Barrier Reef, the second largest barrier reef in the world. A barrier reef is an intricate and exotic system of tiny animals called coral. Each coral is itself an intricate and exotic system of coral polyps, soft-bodied animals that secrete a hard skeleton of calcium carbonate in which to live. These hard coral skeletons form ridges along the coastline in Belize called coral reefs, often associated with lagoons of sea grass and mangrove trees. Coral reefs provide habitat to an exotic array of plants and animals. In 2003, we were there to explore and study how this intricate and exotic ecosystem functioned.

Our orientation to the field station there and the island itself (about two miles long and two miles wide) consisted of a few simple rules:

1. Check your pants for scorpions before putting them on in the morning—we learned this lesson the hard way.
2. Catch only the fish you want to eat, the day you want to eat it because refrigeration was in short supply.
3. Turn off porch lights at night during sea turtle breeding season so that the sea turtle hatchlings would not be distracted and disoriented by the artificial light.
4. Take short showers, just once a day. All the water we had for showers came from rain collected in rain barrels and we didn't know how much it would rain during our stay.

We learned this last lesson the hard way as well. About halfway through our two-week stay on Calabash Caye, we ran out of water for showers, not only because it didn't rain, but also because some of the students took longer than necessary showers and/or showered more often than we agreed. Being from the United States, they believed water came from a faucet, and as long as there was a faucet, there would be water. When I told them we were out of water for showers, they said, "But what will we do?! We can't not shower. I guess we have to go home." I reminded them we couldn't leave the island until the boat from the mainland came for us, and in the meantime, we would just have to wait until it rained until we could shower again.

It seems to me that these rules for living on Calabash Caye are pretty good rules for life in general, and not only on a small island in the middle of a barrier reef, but for life on an even larger island—our island home earth, spinning in the middle of a vast solar system.

The theologian Sallie McFague writes of some new house rules for us to live by; she calls them

God's House Rules.[1] If the whole of creation is God's house, then we must abide by God's house rules, she says, and describes them as such:

1. Take only your share,
2. Clean up after yourselves,
3. Keep the house in good repair for future housemates.[2]

These pretty much sum up the rules we needed to live by on Calabash Caye. They also remind me of three other simple rules, the general rules that are foundational to our Methodist heritage and tradition.

When John Wesley, the founder of the Methodist movement, first began to form societies of Methodists in 1739, the first Methodists decided they needed some rules. Not bad rules or too many rules, but a few good rules. They asked Wesley to come up with some rules for Methodist societies. John Wesley came up with what has been described as Three Simple Rules,[3] which fall into three categories:

1. Do no harm.
2. Do good.
3. Attend upon the ordinances of God or, "stay in love with God," as described by Bishop Reuben Job.[4]

It is important to note that Wesley's examples about doing no harm aren't only about avoiding harming others or ourselves, they are also about not participating in systems that harm others.

Take for example the coral reef I described in Belize. Coral reefs are intricate, delicate, complex ecosystems, teeming with a dazzling array of plants and animals. The barrier reef in Belize we were studying is valuable in and of itself, but we weren't only studying its intrinsic value. Worldwide, coral reefs have tremendous economic value to humans as well, providing important ecological goods and services.

Ecological goods and services are the economic, cultural, and health-related benefits that healthy, well-functioning ecosystems provide to humans. Coral reefs are teeming not only with life but also these ecological goods and services. They are the breeding and nursery grounds for many species of fish, which are important for commercial and recreational fisheries. The National Oceanic and Atmospheric Administration (NOAA) estimates the commercial value of U.S. fisheries from coral reefs to be more than $100 million, and in some places, supply over 50 percent of the fish caught locally for food.[5] Coral reefs are also important for ecotourism worldwide; for example, NOAA estimates that more than 4 million people visit the coral reefs of the Florida Keys each year, spending over $1 million annually.[6] In other parts of the world, this ecotourism can account for almost 90 percent of new economic development.[7] Additionally, coral reefs are important buffers along shorelines, protecting coastal areas from waves, storms, and floods. Finally, coral reefs have been called the medicine cabinets of the twenty-first century, as animals and plant species found there are used for medicinal purposes to treat illnesses such as cancer, arthritis, infections, and viruses.[8]

Yet, these coral reefs are also canaries in a coal mine, signals of what happens when an ecosystem is no longer healthy or functioning well. If we lose coral reefs, we don't just lose a beautiful ecosystem, we lose all the benefits and ecological goods and services. Overfishing, habitat destruction, and climate change are all destroying coral reefs worldwide at an alarming rate. Of particular concern is ocean acidification, the increasing acidity of the surface ocean water. It occurs when carbon dioxide is absorbed by the ocean and changes its pH. The change in the pH of surface ocean water since the beginning of the Industrial Revolution represents approximately a 30 percent increase in acidity.[9] The corals of

Belize and around the world are not able to secrete their calcium carbonate skeletons in these acidic conditions, meaning that the very foundation of these ecosystems is undermined.

While I would never intentionally harm a coral reef—I took great care while snorkeling in Belize to not disturb the reef or its inhabitants—ultimately the amount of energy I use while at home and where that energy comes from impacts the health of coral reefs.

Another example of not participating in systems of harm involves the amount and availability of fresh water for all. Only 0.02 percent of the global water supply is available to humans around the world as surface water or accessible groundwater. Twenty-five percent of the world's population does not have access to fresh water. Water scarcity is an ecological problem—water is diverted from rivers, lakes, and streams for irrigation, industrial use, and consumption. I may not have been the person to use the last bit of water for showers on Calabash Caye, but our institutional water practices are essentially the equivalent of that for 1.5 billion people on the planet.

The Reverend Dean Snyder of Foundry United Methodist Church in Washington, D.C., preached a sermon series on the Three Simple Rules and also tried to live them during the series. He concluded after trying to do no harm for a week that he is personally not very optimistic about doing no harm. Getting through a week, or even a day, without doing any harm to others or ourselves is very hard. In the end, Snyder wonders if it is possible to live in America and to do no harm to creation.[10] Perhaps our focus needs to be on becoming more aware of the harm we do. And to then do less of it.

What if we took these rules seriously, and what if we took them seriously not only for ourselves, and each other, but *for all of God's creation*? What

would that look like, and how would that allow us to do even less harm, even more good, and be in even more relationship with God?

On the small, remote island of Calabash Caye, the rules were even more necessary. In our privileged, North American culture we have the luxury of breaking the rules without ever really feeling the consequences. On Calabash, you either followed the rule to conserve water or you didn't have any water to shower. Water is a gift from the heavens to be conserved and preserved and treated with respect. Our welfare was tied to it. In our society, water isn't so much a gift as it is an expectation from the faucet. There's either too little or too much of it at any given time, and we go through elaborate and expensive measures to control it, to make it serve us, and do with it whatever we please.

The average American uses 80–100 gallons of water a day, compared to the average person in a developing country who uses less than 50 gallons a day. Most of the water Americans use is flushed down the toilet (literally), used for showers/bathing, or to water lawns and golf courses. Americans live under an illusion of water abundance, explains writer Cynthia Barnett in her book *Blue Revolution: Unmaking America's Water Crisis.*[11] Water is no longer the "essence of life but the emblem of luxury."[12] The distance, she writes, between Americans and our global neighbors is about one-third of an acre—the average size of the American lawn—underscoring that the problem is not that there isn't enough water to drink, but that "there isn't enough water to waste."[13] America's "bottlemania" is another example of our disconnection with water. We have bought into the hype that we must buy water that has been bottled by private companies at nearly three thousand times the price of tap water.[14] Only people who view water as a commodity and a luxury would pay that kind of markup for what used to be viewed as the source and essence of life.

So, consider again the rules, John Wesley's or Sallie McFague's, for how we are to be in relationship with one another, with creation, and with God. These rules need not be felt as onerous or burdensome; they are an invitation to live in relationship and abundant life with one another, with creation, and with God. This is the invitation we receive when God calls us to be good stewards of God's creation, to be co-creators with God here on earth. Theologian Norman Habel suggests that before God calls humans to be co-creators, God first calls the earth itself to co-create with God.[15] In Genesis 1:11, God says, "Let the earth put forth vegetation." And the earth does. Habel describes the potential life forces within earth emerging as plant and animals of all kinds. Earth along with God is a "source of all living things . . . earth is the source, home, and haven of living creatures. *Earth is a co-creator with Elohim*"[16] (emphasis added).

A'dam is then created from *adamah* (ground)— the earthling from the earth, with bodies that are approximately two-thirds water, just as the earth is two-thirds water (which may cause us to ask why our planet isn't called "Water" instead of "Earth"). We are earth and water made alive by the breath of God. Two-thirds of the water in our bodies is water from our local drinking water source, underscoring our connection to the waters in our communities, and our brothers and sisters of those communities, with that very connection flowing through our veins. God creates by bringing into relationship. We are created in the image of God out of the dust of the earth.

Dr. Calvin DeWitt, a scientist who is often referred to as the modern-day father of Christian environmentalism, describes the beauty, majesty, and splendor of creation through what he calls the Seven Provisions of the Creator. His training as a scientist helps him understand the processes that make life possible on earth; scriptures such as Psalm 104 and hymns such as "How Great Thy

Art" help DeWitt appreciate the hand of the Creator in this creation. He has spent much of his time studying the biosphere, "the great envelope of life that embraces the face of the earth, what we and all God's creatures inhabit."[17] The biosphere relies upon the cycles in creation, which he describes as the Seven Provisions of the Creator:

1. **Earth's energy exchange with the sun and space:**[18] The sun radiates immense amounts of energy in all directions, including our direction here on earth. It energizes nearly everything on earth, from plants and the animals that eat them, to wind and water patterns across the planet, to automobiles and appliances and the commerce they support. The earth, too, also radiates energy, and the earth's energy balance, or its temperature, depends on how much energy the earth either loses or gains. The earth's temperature is what determines how habitable the planet is, and to support life, as we know it on earth, this temperature must remain relatively constant. The earth's atmosphere, the protective layer of air in between the earth and the sun and the rest of outer space, serves many functions, one of which is to regulate the earth's energy exchange. It also provides the air we breathe. The atmosphere comprises gases, called greenhouse gases, that produce the greenhouse effect, which balances how much energy the earth gains from the sun with how much energy it gives off, or loses. Change these gases, and we change the very processes that regulate our ability to exist on earth.

2. **Soil building:**[19] It is a "veritable symphony of processes" that turns bare rock and landscapes into a medium that can eventually support life.[20] Soil interacts with climate, rainfall, and organisms, and over time becomes richer in nutrients and more supportive of life. Organic plant and animal

matter decay and decompose naturally over long periods of time, adding nutrients to the soil. Soil is further produced and enriched as rocks and sand are weathered. All this takes time and patience; it can take a hundred years to form one inch of topsoil.[21] And yet we know that soil can be lost in only a fraction of that time and with it, our ability to produce enough food for communities locally and globally.

3. **Cycling and recycling in the biosphere:**[22] This includes the carbon cycle, the hydrologic or water cycle, and the nitrogen cycle. These are but a few of the ways in which the biosphere uses and reuses the various substances contained in soil, water, and air to maintain its living and nonliving parts.[23] As living organisms interact with their nonliving environment, ecosystems are formed, and these ecosystems rely on the cycles in creation. Oceans, forests, wetlands, deserts, and prairies are all examples of ecosystems, making up "the biggest ecosystem of them all, the biosphere, the symphony of all symphonies."[24] All the processes that make life on earth possible "continue to bring forth life from death as they cycle and recycle the basic stuff of creation, all powered by our star, the sun."[25] Disruptions to these processes disrupt this symphony, with entire sections playing off-key.

4. **Water purification and detoxification:**[26] Not only is water available and abundant in God's creation, but the flow of that water throughout the biosphere and the earth's ecosystems is also part of the creation. As water flows throughout the earth, it travels through natural filtering systems, such as through rock and soil, or wetlands and marshes. This ecosystem service is provided free of charge, a service that is continually provided, and one we must take care to not overload or interrupt.

5. **Fruitfulness and abundant life:**[27] Life exists from the depths of the oceans where no sunlight reaches, to the heat inside volcanoes, to the cold of below freezing temperatures, to lakes of acid, to the stratosphere six miles above the ground. Even in places where human reason says life should not exist, God's will says yes it can. Scientists today estimate there are nearly 40 million species of living creatures, and yet we have named less than two million,[28] with millions of others becoming extinct before we ever knew they existed.

6. **Global circulations of water and air:**[29] The tilt and rotation of our earth means seasonal and daily changes in when and how much warmth the planet receives, and these differences don't just mean summer and winter, day and night. They also account for the flow of water and air around the earth, circulating oxygen, water vapor, and carbon dioxide, providing for the "breath of life on a planetary scale."[30]

7. **Human ability to learn from creation:**[31] *Adam* from *adamah* was created in the image of God. As DeWitt writes, "This provision allows us to adopt the mind of Christ, learning from the book of God's world and the book of God's works, to safeguard the integrity of creation and sustain and renew the life of the earth, in harmony with God's love for the world."[32]

These seven provisions describe the processes that make life possible on earth, the diversity and abundance of these life forms made possible, and intricate nature of life in general. They describe, to put it succinctly, life in relationship. We as humans find our personhood in relationship to the source of our lives, namely God, and in relationship with the rest of God's creation. What does it mean to be in relationship? Jewish philosopher Martin Buber's essay "I and Thou" addresses questions about how one relates to God, other people, and nature.[33] In the I-It relationship as he describes it, humans experience something. Humans are the subject in this relationship, and nature is the object.

Humans encounter something in the second type of relationship he describes as the I-Thou relationship.[34] It is not a subject and object relationship based on experience, as in the I-It relationship. It is a subject and subject relationship that is mutual and reciprocal.

Archbishop Desmond Tutu describes this mutual relationship, known as Ubuntu, when he says, "I am, because we are; and since we are, therefore I am." The conservationist John Seed puts it this way, "I am part of the rainforest protecting myself. I am that part of the rainforest recently emerged into thinking."[35]

Creation Groaning and Justice for All

Yet we know this creation is groaning, that things are not as they should be. The relationship God desires with all of creation is broken.

What is our ecological crisis? Why is creation groaning? Oil spills, acid rain, global warming, deforestation, extinction, water pollution, and weapons proliferation are all signs of the crisis. DeWitt juxtaposes the Seven Provisions of the Creator[36] with the Seven Degradations of Creation:[37]

1. Changes in the earth's energy exchange with the sun that results in climate change and destruction of the ozone layer, which shields the earth from harmful radiation.[38]

2. Land degradation that reduces available land for creatures and crops and destroys land by erosion, development, and desertification.[39] In some places in the United States, two bushels of topsoil are lost to every one bushel of food harvested, or approximately 60 million tons.[40] Much more topsoil is lost in the sense that it is contaminated by "peacetime pesticides"—chemicals adapted from WWII weapons technology deemed safe after the war for commercial and industrial agricultural uses.

3. Deforestation and habitat destruction that removes approximately 30 million acres each year and degrades an equal amount by overuse.[41] Pavement is added to pavement, and God's house here on earth is reduced to manufactured houses and houses of worship with all the trappings of our commercial lifestyles.

4. Water-quality degradation that (directly or indirectly) pollutes groundwater, lakes, rivers, and oceans.[42] Water is no longer clean or plentiful, and we can no longer safely fish, swim, or be baptized in our local water source.

5. Species extinction[43] that is occurring at a rate nearly 1,000 times the "natural" or "background" rate, meaning as many as 150–200 species go extinct each day, according to the UN Environment Programme.[44]

6. The spread of chemicals, such as DDT, by global circulation patterns, which has resulted in global toxification.[45]

7. Cultural degradation that threatens and eliminates knowledge within indigenous communities about how to live sustainably and cooperatively with creation.[46]

Going back to the Three Simple Rules, how do we stay in love with God? We stay in love with God's creation. We honor and respect the Seven Provisions of the Creator, we do no harm to them, and we do good for ourselves and others by living within them. We reject the false idolatry that tells us we know what we need to live better than God, that we know how the earth should be better than the earth. And we don't just do this because we are concerned about our own basic necessities, about having enough food and water and shelter (which we rightly should be concerned about). We do this because we love God, and this is how we show our faithfulness; demonstrate our love for God.

Ecological awareness, therefore, becomes not a matter of preserving limited natural resources in order to maintain the standard of living to which we have grown accustomed. Hence, the American students' reaction to no water for showers in Calabash Caye. Ecological awareness is not just a matter of democratic fairness—it is justice for all, including the earth and *all* its inhabitants.[47]

I believe our current attitudes toward creation come from a misunderstanding and misuse of the creation stories, an ignorance of ecological themes in other books of the Hebrew Bible, theology based on outdated science, and science based on flawed theology. This has resulted in justifying the domination and exploitation of creation for humanity's purposes. If this is how we have ended up in our current ecological crisis, then we can become part of the ecological solution in several ways. One, we can engage in a careful exegesis of the creation stories. Two, we can combine ecological principles throughout the Hebrew Bible with liberation theology, feminist theology, eschatology, and a doctrine of the Trinity. This will provide a richer theological framework with which to view an ecological theology. Three, we can draw upon the most recent scientific thinking that is evolutionary, relational, unpredictable, holistic, and interdependent. This new cosmology is convergent with an ecological ethic.

When I was the Anacostia Riverkeeper, I was a public advocate for the river and all the communities that live, work, and play in its watershed. I was dubbed the Reverend Riverkeeper, because I wanted the river to be fishable, swimmable, and baptizable. I tried to understand firsthand and in my own community the current environmental crisis and the role of Christians in address-

ing it. The Anacostia River runs through the nation's capital and through the poorest neighborhoods in the city. The communities along its riverbanks bear the brunt of the negative health effects of toxic sites, polluted runoff, and trash. Long before being designated as one of the ten dirtiest rivers in America, the Anacostia used to be the site of baptisms for the African-American churches along its banks. The healing powers of the river are long gone, and the river is in desperate need of healing of its own.

The water that flows in the Anacostia is part of the earth's water cycle. The Bible study *Sacred Waters* from the National Council of Churches EcoJustice Working Group beautifully describes this water cycle:

> The water cycle vividly demonstrates the interrelatedness and deep connections within God's Creation. What affects the air affects the rivers. What affects the rivers affects the oceans. What happens upstream affects life downstream.[48]

Poet and farmer Wendell Berry puts it this way, "Do unto those downstream as you would have those upstream do unto you."[49]

The National Council of Churches *Sacred Waters* study for congregations illustrates how the psalmists understood water as a gift, a gift to all of creation.[50] Their verses tell the story of how water works in creation and the diversity of forms it takes. It is an amazing system, and the cycle water travels is as much God's creation as the water itself. We are part of this cycle, and where we live is where we interact with the water cycle; this is called a watershed.[51] A watershed is an area of land upon which all the rain that falls in that area drains into one body of water. This watershed is our home and home to God's creatures. We are part of this cycle and this cycle is part of us.

Yet, we know this cycle is out of balance somehow as we hear stories of and experience flooding in some areas and drought in others. While some areas have plenty of clean, available drinking water, others have little or none. We build dams and levies to control the flow of water, and we allow harmful chemicals to change the very nature of water. Water that used to flow gently over lush vegetation into streams now roars harshly across asphalt and pours into streams, eroding their banks in the process. The psalmists' vision of how things should be is not how things are, and we know our action, or inaction, is a direct cause. We seem to think we know better than water how water should be water; how water should travel through God's creation; and since God created the waters and the water cycle, we think we know better than God how water should be water.[52] We are created in God's image to be co-creators along with the God of creation. But when we impose our will on creation, we deny God's will and follow our own instead.

In my home, the Anacostia watershed, polluted runoff is a serious threat; it is a sign that this watershed and this home are not well. With so much of the watershed covered by hard pavement instead of grass or trees, water runs across the pavement, picking up sediment and chemicals and trash and carries them into the Anacostia. The water picks up speed as it rolls across the pavement, too, and this erodes the riverbanks, banks that used to be lined with trees or wetlands or other natural buffers. Every year, two billion gallons of polluted runoff carrying trash, sewage, and toxic chemicals enter the Anacostia River. Two-thirds of the brown bullhead catfish in the Anacostia have cancerous lesions or sores, and anyone who eats these catfish also ingests the toxins in their flesh.

That's the bad news. The good news is that we can help return the water cycle to its natural rhythm. We can allow water to be water, to be that for which God created it to be.

Gus Speth, former dean of the Yale School of Forestry and the Environment, said when speaking to a group of pastors:

> Thirty years ago, I thought that with enough good science, we would be able to solve the environmental crisis. I was wrong. I used to think the greatest problems threatening the planet were pollution, bio-diversity loss and climate change. I was wrong there, too. I now believe that the greatest problems are pride, apathy and greed. And for that we need a spiritual and cultural transformation. And we scientists don't know how to do that. We need your help.[53]

Where can that spiritual and cultural transformation come from? It comes from remembering that we are created in God's image from the dust of the earth. From that understanding, we can address the environmental issues that affect the Anacostia River in particular and creation in general. Advances in modern scientific and theological thinking will also help inform a new ecological ethic. In other words, we can follow the rules, the simple rules from John Wesley (do no harm, do good, stay in love with God) to Sallie McFague (take only your share, clean up after yourselves, keep the house in good repair for future housemates), to Jesus Christ (love God with all your heart, mind, and soul, and love your neighbor as yourself). Remember: They are called *simple* rules, not *easy* rules. We, and the earth, in whose image we are partly created, can afford nothing less. ✪

Endnotes

1. Sallie McFague, *Life Abundant: Rethinking Theology and Economy for a Planet in Peril* (Minneapolis, MN: Fortress Press, 2000), 14.

2. Ibid., 122.

3. Reuben P. Job, *Three Simple Rules: A Wesleyan Way of Living* (Nashville: Abingdon Press, 2007), 14.

4. Ibid.

5. "Why Are Coral Reefs So Important?" NOAA, accessed May 2, 2015, http://celebrating200years.noaa.gov/foundations/coral/side.html.

6. Ibid.

7. Ibid.

8. Ibid.

9. Ibid.

10. Dean Snyder, "Three Simple Rules" (sermon, Foundry United Methodist Church in Washington, D.C., September 12, 2010), www.foundryumc.org/sermons/2010%20Sermons/09_12_10.html.

11. Cynthia Barnett, *Blue Revolution: Unmaking America's Water Crisis* (Boston: Beacon Press, 2012), 1.

12. Ibid.

13. Ibid., 11.

14. A.K. Streeter, "We Use How Much Water? Scary Water Footprints, Country by Country," Treehugger, June 24, 2009, www.treehugger.com/clean-water/we-use-how-much-water-scary-water-footprints-country-by-country.html.

15. Norman Habel and Shirley Wurst, eds., *The Earth Story in Genesis* (Cleveland: Pilgrim Press, 2001), 35.

16. Ibid., 48.

17. Calvin DeWitt, *Earthwise: A Guide to Hopeful Creation Care*, 3rd ed. (Grand Rapids, MI: Faith Alive Christian Resources, 2011), 23–34.

18. Ibid., 23.

19. Ibid., 26.

20. Ibid.

21. Ibid.

22. Ibid.

23. Ibid., 27.

24. Ibid., 29.

25. Ibid., 30.

26. Ibid.

27. Ibid.

28. Ibid., 31.

29. Ibid.

30. Ibid., 35.

31. Ibid.

32. Ibid., 38.

33. Martin Buber, *I and Thou*, trans. Walter Kaufmann (New York: Free Press: 1971), 1.

34. Ibid.

35. John Seed, "Beyond Anthropocentrism," in *Thinking Like a Mountain: Toward Council of All Beings*, eds. John Seed, Joanna Macy, Arne Naess, and Pat Fleming (Philadelphia: New Society Publishers, 1988), 1.

36. Calvin DeWitt, *Caring for Creation: Responsible Stewardship of God's Handiwork* (Grand Rapids, MI: Baker, 1998), 10.

37. Calvin DeWitt, "Seven Degradations of Creation," in *The Environment and the Christian: What Does The New Testament Have to Teach*, ed. Calvin DeWitt (Grand Rapids, MI: Baker Book House, 1991), 13–23.

38. Ibid., 13.

39. Ibid., 15.

40. Ibid., 17.

41. Ibid., 19.

42. Ibid., 21.

43. Ibid.

44. John Vidal, "UN Environment Programme: 200 Species Extinct Every Day, Unlike Anything Since Dinosaurs Disappeared 65 Million Years Ago," HuffPost Green, August 17, 2010, www.huffingtonpost.com/2010/08/17/un-environment-programme-_n_684562.html.

45. Calvin DeWitt, *Seven Degradations of Creation*.

46. Ibid.

47. Sallie McFague, *Life Abundant: Rethinking Theology and Economy for a Planet in Peril* (Minneapolis, MN: Fortress Press, 2000), 122.

48. Beth Norcross, "Sacred Waters: A 5-Week Adult Christian Education Course," in *Water Stewards: A Toolkit for Congregational Care of Local Watersheds* (Washington, D.C.: National Council of Churches EcoJustice Working Group 2006), 25–40.

49. Catherine Woodiwiss, "Wendell Berry's Earth Day Speech: 'People Who Own The World Outright For Profit Will Have To Be Stopped,'" Climate Progress, April 23, 2012, http://thinkprogress.org/climate/2012/04/23/469392/wendell-berrys-earth-day-speech-people-who-own-the-world-outright-for-profit-will-have-to-be-stopped.

50. Beth Norcross, "Sacred Waters," 25–40.

51. Ibid.

52. Pat Watkins, "Naked Vegetarianism" (sermon, General Board of Church and Society Building, Washington, D.C., January 26, 2011).

53. Richard Cizik, "What If?" in *Love God Heal Earth: 21 Leading Religious Voices Speak Out on Our Sacred Duty to Protect the Environment*, ed. S.G. Bingham (Pittsburgh: St Lynn's Press, 2009), 9.

About the Author

The Reverend Dottie Yunger is a marine biologist and minister, currently serving as associate pastor at Metropolitan Memorial United Methodist Church in Washington, D.C., and lead pastor for the St. Luke's Mission Center. She was commissioned as an elder in the Baltimore-Washington Annual Conference in 2013. She was formerly the executive director of Interfaith Partners for the Chesapeake, and before that, Anacostia Riverkeeper.

Yunger received her bachelor of science in marine biology from the University of Maryland and master of divinity and theological studies with honors from Wesley Theological Seminary. She has also worked as a marine biologist and environmental educator for the Smithsonian Institution, Discovery Channel, and the National Aquarium. She has studied ecosystem modeling and sea turtle conservation, mostly in warm, sunny climates. In 2009, Yunger was awarded the Living Legend Award by Living Classrooms of the National Capitol Region for her work as Anacostia Riverkeeper.

"A Sojourn to Sacredness," Virginia Conference of The United Methodist Church, 2011.
Photo by Pat Watkins

Chapter 6

Climate Injustice: Human Consequences

Norma Dollaga

How sweet the rain is
Falling on my face, kissing me gently
How beautiful the sun is
Brightly shining through the fields
  and mountains
How gentle the wind is
Tenderly reminding me of the Breath of Life.

That's poetic thanksgiving a faithful could utter
A praise to Creation and to God Almighty
But along the streets and city slums
Through the poor and rural villages
The rain and sun and wind
Has another story to be told.

Through the summer and rainy seasons
The poor ones could always be vulnerable
When the rain comes, afraid that there would
  be no homes
When summer comes, the scourging heat
  seems unbearable.

Oh how much do they wish to have a hot broth
Be at home and together feel the rain
  on the roof
But alas, people in the shanties and makeshift
  homes can
But to wish for home, and broth and fun.

by Norma Dollaga

Let Me Share a Story with You

For a Cup of Soup

The story of Rosalie lingers in my mind; it will not leave me until I write her story the way her grandmother narrated it to me.

"Lolo [grandpa], I want to borrow a cup from your kitchen. Our ma'am [teacher in the school] asked us to bring our cup because she is going to feed us." Those were the words of Rosalie the night before she said goodbye to her family for the last time.

Rosalie is a seven-year-old and grade one pupil in Rapu-Rapu. The public school responded to the widespread hunger and poverty on the island with immediate relief like providing soup for school children.

Rapu-Rapu is an island in the Albay Gulf, near Legazpi City, in the Bicol region of the Philippines. It takes twelve hours to travel by land from Manila to reach Legazpi and a three-hour motorboat ride to reach Rapu-Rapu. The island is blessed with natural resources. People live in simplicity. They are farmers and fisherfolk. While waiting for harvest, they turn to the sea to supplement their daily needs. The ordinary people who live on a rich island have experienced many difficulties. Despite this, they have managed to survive.

The land and sea are so rich that the island was coveted by big mining corporations like Lafayette Mining Corporation from Australia. Because the corporation's capital is huge, the government has permitted them to operate without limits to extract the rich resources of the island.

The church and the people have not welcomed the mining corporation as they believe that it will only destroy the environment and affect sources of livelihood. The people will never benefit from their presence since the interest of the corporation is to extract profit for itself, even at the expense of the environment.

In October of 2007, there was a massive fish kill. The community, concerned scientists, the church, and people's organizations all pointed to the Lafayette Mining Corporation as the cause of this catastrophe.

The people rely so much on the land and sea for their living. After the strong Typhoon Reming hit the island in November 2006, all their expected harvests were destroyed. The people turned to the sea as their hope. It had always been their answer to basic food needs. But the sea was poisoned and the fish were affected. No one dared to eat fish coming from the island because of the poison that contaminated both the sea and the fish.

Hunger and sickness, misery and suffering followed. They are now constant companions of the community in Rapu-Rapu.

Rosalie became one of the victims. She is a middle child of seven children. Her father is a construction worker in Manila who sends money only occasionally because of the contractual character of his work. The children live under the care of their mother and paternal grandparents.

On the day of the soup distribution, Rosalie was asked by the teacher to bring out her cup. She went back to the house of her lolo. The house was not too far from the school, which is why her teacher allowed her to go. She stopped just a few steps from the house. Her sister and mother wondered why. She was not able to get home; she fell to the ground. When her mother reached out for her, she was no longer moving or breathing. Her mother kept on calling her name, but Rosalie did not answer, no sound, no tiny voice that would echo her cheerful moods. Rosalie had died.

She died before her time. She was just a child.

Her father was not able to see her body buried because he had no money for transportation. When he arrived home, there were only six tiny children to embrace and welcome him. No more middle child to cling on his back. He missed her smile and innocent laughter.

Her grandmother told me that whenever there is food available, the father divides it equally among the children. The father would stop and burst into tears because the space and the cup of Rosalie is no longer there to receive the food. At sunset, he would look to the sea and tears would roll from his eyes as if wanting to join the large body of water. He does not sob, he does not cry out loud, but the warm tears would keep on flowing until he would lie down to rest.

This is the story of Rosalie, her father, mother, grandmother, grandfather, and siblings.

They say when someone dies, the person either becomes an angel or a star. Maybe Rosalie is both an angel and a star now. She is an angel whispering to my ears to tell her story. She is a star now, reminding the people that there should be no more Rosalies, children of her age who would die of hunger.

We left Rapu-Rapu days before Christmas. And I need to be healed from the pain of such a story. I kept on telling her story to my friends and I do not know if I was spoiling their Christmas celebration. Now, I am writing her story to be connected with her and the millions of children suffering from hunger and poverty.[1]

The story of Rosalie is our story, too. One life is connected with another. Her story is not just about an accidental death or a common belief that it is God's will. It was an untimely death. Her death in a situation of impoverishment amid a wealth of natural resources is an irony in itself.

The Sin of a Profit-Driven Economy: Why Must the Poor Suffer?

Years ago, we used to hear the saying, "When Mother Earth suffers, women suffer too." It suggests that the image of the earth is very much akin to the nature of a woman, giving birth and nurturing her offspring. We have been irresponsible stewards as evidenced by the groaning and pain of creation, as well as our daily experiences, because we are no longer in one accord with the whole creation. In addition to the "we," the earth has been abused by the structural and systemic sins of market-driven economies that contribute to climate change and environmental destruction that affects us all.

First and foremost, the world where we live is not our private property. Our biblical tradition confirms this. The land, sea, air, and sun are not ours to control. It belongs to the Creator (Genesis 1 and 2, Leviticus 25). This world is not yours, it is not ours, and it should not be owned by multinational corporations, by colonial masters, or big landlords. The earth's resources belong to the Creator and we are stewards of God's creation.

The historical emergence of private property paved the way for class ownership, patriarchy, war, colonization, and plunder. The mindless extraction of the earth's resources for profit has violated all the laws of ecological relationships between people and the earth, thus the world's ecosystems are in chaos. The ideology of dom-

ination, rooted in arrogance and resulting in the accumulation of property, makes every gift of natural resources a source of super profit that would only benefit a small class of people. It has wounded the earth, poisoned the sea, contaminated the air, beleaguered the creatures, and displaced and marginalized those whose daily living is in accord with nature. These are our indigenous kith and kin, the farmers and the fisherfolk.

We are in a period when we see natural resources as currency. The monetary profit value of vegetables and fruits is of immediate concern of owners.

> Indeed, under this system (capitalism), goods and services are produced not to fulfill basic human necessities and improve human welfare but to generate business profit. In the words of Bolivian President Evo Morales, "In the hands of capitalism everything becomes a commodity: the water, the soil, the human genome, the ancestral cultures, justice, ethics, death . . . and life itself. Everything, absolutely everything, can be bought and sold under capitalism. And even 'climate change' itself has become a business." People's needs and desires are satisfied only to the extent that they can afford to pay for these commodities.[1]

There is a need for an honest acknowledgment and humble recognition that we do not own the earth's resources, and that the people should enjoy the equal and just sharing of the earth's gifts. Ecological justice is a prerequisite to restore the earth's resources, beauty, and grace.

> However, in accumulating wealth historically and currently and in attaining and maintaining their current standards of living, rich, industrialised nations in the North have used up far more than their fair share of the atmospheric global commons at the expense of the equitable rights of Southern countries. . . . Historically and in the present, climate debt is accumulated in the name of development. Mainstream economic thought and dominant economic systems have

largely reduced the concept of development to mere economic expansion or continuous—even unlimited—growth in production, income and consumption. A fundamental question that we must tirelessly pose is: "Why is the goal of sustainable development... growth in the production of goods and services on environmentally-sustainable terms, instead of growth in the health of persons and the rest of nature in communities within their respective habitats?"[2]

To protect the whole earth is to recognize that we are co-stewards with the Creator and we share the responsibility of cultivating it, not for super profit or gain that would only benefit the tiniest section of the population, but for ensuring that the resources are justly distributed and that the generations to come will enjoy the fruits of creation.

A Native American proverb reminds us, "Treat the earth well: it was not given to you by your parents, it was loaned to you by your children. We do not inherit the Earth from our Ancestors, we borrow it from our children."

This, for me, is a very decent theological formulation. After all, we came from soil (ha-'adamah) and we are of the soil, of the land. From dust we came, to dust we all shall return. It is very interesting to note that even our Filipino tales of origin speak of us coming from the earth. Most tales of origin share a common thread, we come from the ground, from the earth. We are groundlings. We are earthlings.

This is a humbling realization for many. If we came from the earth, then we must know that we are interrelated, that we are interconnected. The earth, sea, wind, and light are teaching us the wisdom of having good relationships. Having a good relationship with one another is having a communion of joy, equal and just sharing of resources, wholeness, peace, and the timeless value of true love and compassion.

Ha–'adamah (from the earth), we homo sapiens (human beings) are part of the whole creation. Among the earth's dwellers we were given the power to think, plan, evaluate, develop, and cultivate the earth for our consumption and satisfaction. We invent tools, instruments, and gadgets for our survival. But when an inappropriate accumulation of things occurs, transforming profit into capital to gain more profit, the harmonious status of the earth's interconnectedness is severely altered.

It is not common knowledge that it is actually the poor who pay the highest price for the environmental destruction, though they are not the main violators of ecological laws.

> The poorest people in the poorest countries who contributed least to climate change are also the first and foremost affected by it. While world leaders are haggling over emission reductions and who will pay for the mitigation and adaptation, millions of the world's poorest populations are daily suffering the consequences of climate change—extreme weather events that destroy crops, livestock and homes, more frequent and prolonged droughts and floods, loss of freshwater supply, increase in pathogens, destruction of marine and coastal resources, ancestral land, food and water insecurity, energy insecurity, and so on.[3]

Of Typhoons and Disasters

Typhoons are innate characters of the natural world. When they strike, they cause traumatic experiences, especially for those who are severely affected by their onslaught. But every typhoon affects communities, people, and the environment only because they have become vulnerable. Let us at least give respect to the typhoons; after all, they are not the creation of the rotting structural system.

People's vulnerabilities most often result from poor government, unequal distribution of resources, and lack of access to and control of

Participants in a cash for work program clean up debris in Tacloban, a city in the Philippines province of Leyte that was hit hard by Typhoon Haiyan in November 2013. The storm was known locally as Yolanda. The ACT Alliance has been active here and in affected communities throughout the region helping survivors to rebuild their homes and recover their livelihoods. *Photo by Paul Jeffrey*

the resources that rightly belong to them. The Philippines has been visited by disaster after disaster. From all these, we have learned that a disaster is not about typhoons and natural forces. Disasters happen because people have become vulnerable to natural forces or human-caused aggression.

And more often it is the poor, those who have been neglected and robbed of basic and social services, who are exposed to multiple layers of vulnerabilities. While it is true that both the rich and poor have been affected by recent typhoons, what's more tragic is that the poorest are the ones who have suffered the most.

Super Typhoons Yolanda and Pablo

On December 3, 2012, super typhoon Pablo (also called Bopha by some agencies) struck the Philippines with sustained winds greater than 240 km/h (149 mph), the equivalent of a Category 5 hurricane in the Atlantic Ocean.

Raging, briskly dancing, setting its own pace, and leaving hundreds of people dead, the typhoon razed infrastructures. It commanded the mortals to show compassion and love, and reminded us all that the emotional attachment to friends and family can be astounding.

The moment of truth comes again, inviting the human community to respond mercifully and justly. Blaming the victims is the most insensitive thing to do. Taking advantage of their misery by imposing value-added taxes, increasing the cost of commodities, and exploiting the situation for a political-electoral campaign is an almost unforgivable sin. Acts of mercy and charity are exceedingly needed. Fortunately, generosity is not hard to find in our country and from people across the world. An act of justice is needed, for the disaster speaks about policies, inequalities, exploitation, environmental plunder, and aggressive development. Justice is hard to find, but it is still possible. However, it would take a social-political overhaul.

Greater Storms than Calamities

Just before the forecast of super typhoon Pablo in late 2012, Mindanao was being devastated not by normal meteorological storms but by storms created by corporate greed, human rights violations, and environmental destruction courtesy of profit-driven mining operations and explorations.

In that year alone, under the watch of the current administration, there were thirty-four environmental justice advocates killed in Mindanao. Twenty-six of them were Lumad indigenous people.

In 2012, 159 anti-mining advocates and human rights defenders were facing trumped-up charges. They were being tagged as insurgents and rebel sympathizers. Indigenous peoples and peasant communities became victims of enforced displacements by military operations that affected thousands of families. Schools became virtual garrisons as military personnel and war equipment were stationed there.[4]

What happened to the Liguyon family is a devastating example of this. Sharon Liguyon and her husband Jimmy Liguyon, a barangay captain (the highest elected official in the community), were strong advocates of environmental protection and were against the intrusion of destructive mining activities and biofuel plantations in their local area. On March 5, 2012, Jimmy Liguyon was shot dead inside their house. At that time he was the vice chairperson of a regional indigenous peoples' group in Mindanao, local church council chairperson of the United Church of Christ in the Philippines, and a datu (tribal elder) of the Matisalog tribe. Sharon and her family were among the internally displaced peoples. She has been seeking justice for her slain husband, but the wheel of justice is not moving.

Mindanao is blessed with natural resources. Its wealth could sustain and nourish its people if the resources were justly shared and if science and technology were appropriated for the welfare of the people and the natural world.

Mindanao is a beautiful island with rich cultures and history. Like millions of other Filipinos and Filipinas, its peoples long for an end to violence and ecological devastation.

While typhoons and calamities are occurrences over which we do not have any control, an unjust structural system can cause equally grave devastation on the people. Laws and policies, and a market-driven economy that caters to the economic interests of big business do not only invite disaster, they are in themselves disasters taking the lives of the people and the capacity of nature to provide for the needs of all. Those who advocate creation care are killed, harassed, and tagged as supporters of the revolutionary movement, and in the present context are considered by the state to be terrorists. The truth is, communities are suffering and become disintegrated even if they do not oppose development aggression. People are driven away, displaced from their sources of livelihood, even as young children are killed, and boys and girls are denied access to proper education.

This is the storm, destructive and deadly.

Typhoon Pablo may leave us mourning the dead, lamenting the destruction our eyes have witnessed. Another typhoon may come, as it is part of nature. We cannot command the typhoon, but we can lessen the vulnerability of the people. Typhoons come and go, and generosity is tested in times of its visits. But there is a storm greater than a typhoon—injustice, inequality, exploitation, and development aggression.

As It Was in Pablo, so in Yolanda (Haiyan)

Super typhoon Yolanda (also called Haiyan) is considered to be the most powerful storm recorded in history to hit the island of Visayas. It left the country with more than six thousand people dead, devastated infrastructure, destroyed homes and buildings, damaged the economic resources of the people, and sent the poor into an unspeakable state of poverty.

Climate change, typhoons, and natural calamities are normal occurrences that visit our country. Yet when they strike, injustice is exposed. Obviously it is the poor, victims of unjust rules, exploitation, and chronic patronage politics that are the most vulnerable. Chronic poverty, economic injustice, and market and business interest development increase the vulnerability of the poor. Likewise, the government is directly accountable for the unabated plunder of natural resources, like large-scale mining and extraction, logging, and the foreign plunder of natural wealth.

The eastern Visayas region, particularly the provinces of Leyte and Samar, were the worst hit by Typhoon Yolanda. The region is the second poorest region next to the Autonomous Region in Muslim Mindanao.

The Impact of the Suffering Earth on Local People

A research study entitled "Climate Change and Gender Justice: A Participatory Research Study on the Impact of Climate Changes on Women," reveals the impact of climate change on women in three selected rural communities in the Philippines. Women observed the impact of climate change on agriculture, biodiversity, women, and families. No rain means the loss of agricultural seeds. When seeds do not germinate, there is a total loss of yields. Many farmers are also heavily indebted. The loan interest-rate increases if they cannot pay on time. When rain comes after a prolonged drought, they could plant but lower yields are expected due to insect infestations. Likewise, massive soil erosion decreases the field's fertility.[5]

The number of farming hours has been reduced due to increasing temperatures over the last two decades. Previously, farmers could work 11 hours in the field (5:00 a.m.–12:00 p.m and 1:00 p.m.–6:00 p.m.), but now they can only work for five to six hours (6:00 a.m.–9:00 a.m. and 4:00 p.m.–6:00 p.m.). This, of course, impacts the harvests.

Reduced crop production means less income for families. It is not a surprise that children stop attending school because of lack of resources. Adult members of the families (mothers, fathers) are forced to work off of the farm. Some become scavengers, women do service work (household help), laundry work, and dishwashing in food establishments.

However, the peasant women try to find alternatives to mitigate the impact of climate change. They are able to address the impact of climate change in immediate ways. They use multicropping methods, green manuring (weeds and grasses that grow in the farm are left to rot on the soil to increase the fertility of the soil), and they plant fruit trees and bamboo grass to prevent soil erosion, keeping the traditional farming practices of the indigenous people (Dumagats). The women have learned the Dumagat's way of planting and caring for the earth. One of these traditions is keeping the seeds of rice, corn, fruit, and vegetables. It is a way to preserve the variety of fruit and grains. Likewise the propagation of herbal plants is being accomplished.

Even with these efforts, the farmers are still insecure as land tenure poses a threat and risk to the potential for sustaining, strengthening, and expanding these adaptation strategies.

The Risk of Taking the Side of Climate Justice

Father Fausto "Pops" Tentorio served the indigenous people in Mindanao beginning in 1978 and was the head of the Tribal Filipinos Apostolate of the Diocese of Kidapawan. He was a humble missionary who opted to work with the poor indigenous people and advocate for their struggle for development and environmental protection. He promoted sustainable agriculture and community-oriented, capacity-building development programs. He had been with the Lumad communities and became a voice against military operations. In a statement about Tentorio, the Promotion of Church People's Response (PCPR) wrote, "His life, works and ministry have been welcomed and embraced by the tribal communities. The mastermind who ordered the firing of the bullets that killed him has sacrificed him on the altar of injustice and hate."[6]

Tentorio was gunned down on the morning of October 17, 2011, by a helmet-wearing, motorcycle-riding gunman, believed to be an element of the Armed Forces of the Philippines.

The Kapatirang Simbahan Para sa Bayan (KASIMBAYAN) and the Promotion of Church People's Response felt the loss of a priest and a prophet in our current time: We join the indigenous people, the human rights activists, the environmentalists, the young people whom he encouraged to get an education, the children who are students of the schools he supported to build, his religious congregation, and the many people who share his commitment.

We give Fr. Fausto "Pops" Tentorio, PIME (Pontifical Institute for Foreign Missions) the highest honor worthy of a martyr. He lived out the missionary imperative of loving his neighbor and serving the least of our brothers and sisters. His life was never wanting of commitment but overwhelming in simplicity.

Tentorio represents the meaning of international solidarity. A foreigner who lived in a first-world country but chose to travel miles away to fulfill a service of offering one's self for the sake of others. His mission broke the barriers of race, class, and religion to reach out to those who have been made *anawim* (poor who depend on God) by a system. His mission reflects that across the world, anawim share common suffering and dreams. He spoke their language and shared the heartbeat of their struggles and hopes.

We cherish his life and celebrate the ministry he shared with the people. We convey our deepest sympathy to the PIME congregation who allowed their brother Fr. "Pops" Tentorio to be where his heart, soul, mind and strength could be attuned with the longings, aspirations and vision of the people, particularly the indigenous people in Mindanao.

We share the pain with the indigenous people whom he held dearly in his heart. We lost a man whose sincere commitment was manifested in his life and work. His death was as untimely as the untimely deaths of all the victims of extrajudicial killings. It sends a chilling message that those who work for environmental protection, alternative livelihood for the indigenous peoples, rights and dignity of the national minorities, against militarization and transnational corporate mining live a risky life. The killing itself has sown terror and fear among those who pursue the righteous causes of the people and environment. It is sad that impunity happens over and over under the current administration of President Benigno Aquino.

There are many whose lives have been sacrificed in defense of God's creation. There are church people who by imperative of their faith have taken the risks of pursuing the cause of justice, including supporting environmental protection and resisting development aggression.

KARAPATAN, a human rights organization in the Phillipines, has reported an increasing rate of extrajudicial killings and human rights violations against environmentalists and those who oppose extractive and large-scale mining. From 2010–

2013, there were six environmentalists, thirty-seven indigenous people, and ninety-eight peasants who became victims of extrajudicial killings.[7]

Conclusion

What values do we uphold and which life-path are we treading? To care for the earth takes a strong commitment. To care for the earth is not the end itself. We need to take care of the Creator's resources so that people can live fully as human beings. Humans are to enjoy the land, seas, wind, and light not according to their capacity to purchase, but according to the moral and ethical standards for the enjoyment of these gifts. As a community of people, we must have full participation in laying out plans, decisions, and actions as to how those resources will be properly used and appropriated.

We should also look at problems from a wider perspective. As Christians, we must follow a disciplinary rule of administering resources. Individual initiatives are important, but we also need to address the economic, political, and cultural structures that promote the destruction of the earth's resources.

As individuals we do our share, but private lifestyle changes are not enough. If we limit ourselves to such schemes, the powers-that-be will continue unabated with their greed.

We have to collectivize our efforts and as organized communities and groups register our prophetic judgment.

The standard of this world says the World Trade Organization policies are good, globalization will result in economic wealth, break down all obstacles to development, and lead us to further progress. There is no other way to go but through globalization.

Genuine redistribution and ecological sustainability, however, require tremendous political will as well as a radical change in mainstream economic thinking and the values that undergird it. (Are competition and materialism Christian values?) In short, genuine redistribution and ecological sustainability demand a paradigm shift, which entails challenging the status quo and dominant political and economic powers. Needless to say, this is a tough order. An engaged, critical and active global civil society—justice and peace networks and youth movements—founded in solidarity with each other will be pivotal in agitating for much-needed transformations. Already the seeds of change lie within rural and coastal communities and youth, indigenous women's organisations that are facing up to the challenges posed by the global financial crisis, economic and ecological crises through a wide range of actions: agricultural adaptation, awareness-building, community organisation and political advocacy. We must support and nourish this cause for hope.[8]

And so our environment is suffering; we witness its dying state and hope for resurrection. But the wealth of the forests, the mountains, and the seas can not be resurrected in a matter of three days. Scientists say that it will take time, a long time, before nature can regenerate and replenish itself.

With healthy activist lifestyles, we should be engaged in organized action that would confront and challenge institutions and world economic systems that remain enemies of the environment.

The human community must decide how to nurture the earth's resources and how to work in harmony with nature. As people, we must assume the responsibility of stewardship for today and the ages that all may enjoy abundant life. Justice is a basic requirement. ✪

Endnotes

1. Paul L. Quintos and John Paul Corpus, *Primer on the Climate Crisis Roots and Solutions* (Quezon City, Philippines: Ibon Foundation, 2010), 13.

2. Athena Peralta, "The Copenhagen Accord: A Failure to Deliver Climate Justice and Recognise Climate Debt," *YMCA World 1*, (March 2010), 5–6.

3. Paul L. Quintos, "Climate Funds and Justice," *Reality Check* (April 2009), 4.

4. Mindanao People's Statement, *"Tama Na! Sobra Na! Stop the Killings! Stop Largescale Mining!"* petition, http://apenews.org/news_read.asp?nid=396.

5. "Climate Change and Gender Justice: A Participatory Research Study on the Impact of Climate Change on Women in Three Selected Rural Communities in the Philippines," PAN Asia Pacific, February 28, 2013, www.panap.net/en/fs/post/food-sovereignty/2397.

6. The Promotion for Church People's Response in the Philippines, "Statement on the Ruthless Killing of Fr. Fausto Tentorio, PIME," October 18, 2011, http://nychrp.info/2011/10/18/statement-on-the-ruthless-killing-of-fr-fausto-tentorio-pime.

7. "2013 Karapatan Year-End Report on the Human Rights Situation in the Philippines," Amnesty International Deutschland, accessed May 18, 2015, www.amnesty-philippinen.eu/2013%20KARAPATAN%20YEAREND%20REPORT.pdf.

8. Athena Peralta, "Poverty, Wealth & Ecology," World Student Christian Federation, Asia-Pacific Region, accessed May 18, 2015, www.wscfap.org/resources/perspectives/2009/2009-peralta_poverty.html.

About the Author

Deaconess Norma Dollaga is the general secretary of KASIMBAYAN, a national ecumenical organization in the Philippines doing education on peace, justice, and human rights. She is a deaconess of the Manila Episcopal Area of The United Methodist Church. She is a graduate of Harris Memorial College in Rizal, Philippines, an institution founded by women foreign missionaries to train deaconesses in the Philippines. Dollaga worked in local churches as a Christian education deaconess and is currently a lecturer of gender studies at Harris Memorial College. She is very much involved in the ministry of empowering women, justice, peace, and human rights. Dollaga has been immersed and is continuously immersing herself in the communities and organizations of peasants, indigenous peoples, migrants, the urban poor, and workers, where she gathers so much strength and inspiration from their struggles and unbending hope.

Preparing to enter the People's Climate March, New York City, September 2014.
Photo by Pat Watkins

Chapter 7

Climate Justice: What Needs to Happen?

Kathleen Stone

Then the angel showed me the river of the water of life, bright as crystal, flowing from the throne of God and of the Lamb through the middle of the street of the city. On either side of the river is the tree of life with its twelve kinds of fruit, producing its fruit each month; and the leaves of the tree are for the healing of the nations.

—Revelation 22:1–2

What a vision John shares in the book of Revelation! John was living in the midst of the destructive Roman occupation, under the constant threat of militarism and rising political and economic tension when he had this vision. He had witnessed the attack on the Holy of Holies (the Temple). The world was falling down around him; such a vision would have been unlikely unless it came from the very heart of God.

In the middle of the devastating concern of interlocking crises we've faced, in the food crisis, the economic crisis, the climate crisis, the growing political/economic divide, and diminishment of the average person's power and participation, injustice appears to have grown deeper and more pervasive. And because of this, the church needs to more powerfully model a way of doing it differently. To be the deep-hearted tree of life, flowing from a crystal river, whose fruit comes forth every day and whose leaves are for the healing of the nations, in this day and age, will not happen without intentional resistance to those things

that are continuing to produce such crises, and it will not happen without intentional choice to be those things that align with God's vision of community and care and justice.

We Need to Renew the Vision of the "Good God Life"

We need to renew John's vision of the good life, which is birthed from God's vision of a good and just community. This vision stands in remarkable contrast with the world's vision of "the good life," whose foundation is the acquisition of material goods. This constant background news of "getting and spending"[1] has saturated our airwaves, our minds, and our behaviors and is simply not sustainable; it is exploitative of the earth and its people. And so we need to envision an economy that transforms this to a system that encourages us to be in community with one another and in relationship with a planet, which desperately needs love to be its rule. To believe that there is a way to realize this vision may be the hardest transformation we make.

Churches, through their relief work, are on the front lines when climate disaster hits. When Hurricane Sandy, Hurricane Katrina, Typhoon Haiyan, or large tornadoes in the Midwest or Southern United States, or major floods, droughts, or other environmental disasters strike, the church is there struggling along with the people in every community. The local churches feed, house, and become local centers of care to those who are hurting. We are heartbroken when we see such suffering, and we will do almost anything to help. This is amazing God-centered work and the sacrifice and love exemplified in these actions are certainly born from a vision of God's love.

But, churches also need to be centers of organizing against the systemic and root causes of such suffering. We need to be those who put our hands and hearts to building the stuff that truly makes for life not only today, but for all God's children today and tomorrow. We try to clean up after Hurricane Sandy or Katrina or Typhoon Haiyan, and rebuild homes for some families, reestablish business as usual, but unless we change the root causes of such large storms, what will happen when the next crisis hits and the next one and the next one? We need to build alternatives where caring relationships with the earth and its people are key drivers of the economy so that these root causes of injustice and inattention to environmental sustainability can compost into a new and aligned way of life.

Imagine if the vision that we set forth was so powerful that it focused not only our minds, but organized the work of the many financial and personal resources of the church so that we could build sustainable, economically just, and environmentally sound opportunities! Imagine if this were ministry with those who have long been at the bottom of the economic system. Imagine economic opportunities coming to the fore that reduce greenhouse emissions, save energy, and rebuild ecosystems, which reduce waste, provide good food, and also create jobs that are good for people and the environment!

This transformation will need a vision and it will also need all of our resources, not just our money, but also our time and our understanding of power. It will require true civic participation and equally powered decision-making. The

A United Methodist Women partner at Assembly 2014 was Kentuckians for the Commonwealth. In the heart of coal country—one of the most insidious industrial contributors to climate change—this organization has cast this vision:

We have a vision …

We are working for a day when
Kentuckians — and all people —
enjoy a better quality of life.
When the lives of people and
communities matter before profits.

When our communities have good jobs
that support our families
without doing damage to the water,
air, and land.

When companies and the wealthy pay
their share of taxes
and can't buy elections.

When all people have health care,
shelter, food,
education, and other basic needs.

When children are listened to and valued.

When discrimination is wiped out of our
laws, habits, and hearts.

And when the voices of ordinary people
are heard and respected
in our democracy.[2]

Now that's a tangible vision! Can you see it?

transformation will change our current way of life. It will mean working side-by-side, caring for one another in ways that are substantive and have the potential to form the rewarding, substantially loving, and sustainable communities we thirst for. This is a renewal of current definitions of "the good life."

In 2009, the CEOs of the Cleveland Clinic, Cleveland Foundation, and some universities came together to ask what and how they might provide a sustainable economic development program for the economically depressed areas in Cleveland, Ohio. The Evergreen Cooperatives emerged from this meeting. These cooperatives are a transformative economic model that sustainably addresses issues of food deserts, waste, and energy while also addressing economic injustice by creating both shared ownership and shared profits with their workers.[3] Through building state-of-the-art greenhouses, green laundry facilities, and training opportunities for community members to learn how to install energy efficiency projects, these worker-owned cooperatives are creating incentives to support sustainable ways of life, address urban food deserts, and incentivize a depressed community to prosperity.

Imagine if this was the vision and our focus for possibilities within the church.

Some Paradigms Needing Transformation

There are some ways of thinking that are stumbling blocks to living out a renewed vision that moves us toward transformation. The following paradigms are a few examples:

1. **Financial profit is imperative to living the good life, as is a growth economy.** The industrial economy continues to block the transition to a more fair and sustainable economy because what has incentivized us and encouraged us and what we've set forth in policy to protect our way of life is the notion that profit is imperative. We've truly thought that good-ness and justice will follow. But, they haven't! Goodness and justice must be the roots of the system, not an end result. The emissions from purchases that make up the good life, as the world defines it, support the current system even if it means unjust relationships with the earth and her people. Currently, the international trade system allows companies to pollute land, air, and water so that some increase profits and others can buy more stuff. However there are peoples that suffer disproportionately from these actions, and without a clean environment, become even more impoverished. Polluting the land, air, and water not only deposits more carbon in the atmosphere than the atmosphere can handle, but also leads to the atmosphere's failure to do its amazing work absorbing the greenhouse gases. This belief that financial profit makes the good life is truly anti-gospel thinking! How many biblical chapters and verses are about the priority of love over money? Anything other than love as our root to the good life is ultimately socially, economically, politically, and environmentally unsustainable.

2. **We are independent from one another and can make our own choices.** This is simply not true. Anyone who has lived a bit on this earth knows it takes a village and a world to create the infrastructure upon which we depend. Human beings were never meant to survive as independent units. We know that what hurts one, truly hurts others, and in a wider view of the world, hurts all. Each hurting life hurts others. It's just the way it is. Valuing relationships with those near and far more than profit or convenience needs to be addressed intentionally. We've been going about our business of building our own lives, blind to the injustice to the earth and its inhabitants that our lifestyles cause. Valuing independence is anti-gospel thinking! One need only think of Romans 12 to understand

how deeply we need one another and how deeply we're interconnected.

3. **Efficiency is the best way.** We have worshiped efficiency—getting the most for the least in as little time as possible! Our whole system of industrialization and energy use is built upon this value. This often means that only some have the decision-making power because it's more efficient! Yet, this way has no basis in the Christian gospel. This is not the way God taught us to love. God took time out to come down to earth, to spend time with us, and to stop at people's houses. God is personally involved in the peoples' anxieties and hurts, and God eventually spent the most (Jesus' life) and got little in return. Jesus asked us to be like him—not too busy in the name of efficiency—not refusing Zacchaeus' invitation, the Syrophoenician women's intrusion, the Samaritan woman's or Mary's conversation because he had more important things to do.

There's truly no better community for transforming the above deep paradigms than the community of Jesus Christ, because that is where the gospel breathes.

The gospel is so rich with the good life. With the model of the connectional church, we have the ability to sit nearby and witness those who are right now drowning in the violent consequences of the paradigms above. A polluted stew of air, water, and land surrounds some communities and comes way too near others. We can, with the grace of God, gather around the table, recognize that the current profit system requires extraction, production, and waste zones, which disproportionately affects some people. In the connectional church, we can deepen our relationships and care for the earth and its people by directly relating with those who have experienced historic and current acts of climate injustice the most, and recognize our profound interdependence with them. In the connectional church, we can stop worshiping efficiency and, just like Jesus who sat with those who suffered as a result of an unjust system, we can listen to those who have direct knowledge of what just, healed, and redeemed relationships should look like. If we've succeeded at this system that has hurt so many, the gospel demands that we think this through and accept that the grace of Jesus is sufficient, even as we work hard to change our ways and lives.

The transformation of those of us in the church is a challenge, and we have the deep power of the gospel to root us! Another of the major obstacles

Getting the most for the least in as little time as possible makes no sense in the most fundamental of all orders—that of natural law. If one looks at something like agricultural monocropping, one recognizes the dangers of efficiency. Monocropping was established to increase agricultural output efficiency. Pest control is easier when using chemicals that are specific to pests and not to plants. Certain seeds were developed that were weed-resistant. Chemical fertilizers were developed to get the most output for the least input. However, we now know without a doubt that monocropping and industrial agricultural actually create many times more greenhouse gases than traditional and organic farming methods that value biodiversity. We now also know that tending to the soil in careful ways and the recycling of waste through composting and working with bees, birds, and bugs as natural co-workers can not only help the atmosphere, but also increase production yield and quality. Although this kind of farming takes more time and is deemed less efficient, it naturally sequesters carbon, does not use chemicals, and over time the soil becomes more productive per acre.

we face in this transformation is a renewed political and economic and social culture that truly values the kind of substantive relationships we need.

Besides being contrary to gospel relationships, an individual making the biggest and fastest impact is not a democratic value, it is a capitalistic one. We have to discuss and disagree, and that takes a long time. When you involve those for whom injustice has been an ongoing fact, democracy requires the need for real patience, faithfulness, love, and grace. To break this pattern of independence, efficiency, and profit that runs so deep in our ways of doing things, we need everyone at the table! However, be aware that it will reduce our efficiency. We will need to take time, create longer processes, and have longer meetings, but what a reward! It will raise our true understanding of the diverse experiences in the world, raise our ability to listen to one another, establish a practice of justice, and encourage us to hear the earth and the soil's cries! Loving takes time. And this kind of deep listening to one another and to the earth is love.

Climate change has given us an opportunity as it has pointed to a huge flaw in our industrialized system of development. That which the designers and benefiters in their best intentions thought would genuinely save the world, where everyone would be fed, housed, clothed, and receive health care that would heal the worst of diseases, simply did not work for the earth and for some of its communities, and perhaps all of us. Instead, it has left us with an urgent need to transform ourselves from current exploitative relationships with the natural world and an unjust history of economic exploitation of her communities. The extraction, production, and burning of fossil fuels, which drives the energy that churns out our production, is unsustainable and is creating larger gaps in health, economic, and political access daily. The only way forward is to transform these exploitative relationships with the earth, its ecologies, and among its peoples to relationships that are just, sustainable, and caring.

So, both in gospel and secular terms, if we look at climate change with a mind willing to change to be more gospel-like, more democratic, more just, we can address climate justice concerns. This is how we prepare the soil with the things that are here, and create with its compost the rich deep loam in which God can then plant the tree of life. These are radical changes that call us to resist the ways things are, and root ourselves in a new way so we can be the tree of life.

Our Tools

The church is uniquely situated to model the behaviors that are required in this time of needed urgent transformation:

Presence

The church exists in nearly every community. This is a remarkable gift when we think about transforming a culture. Imagine this fellowship in every city and town developing alternatives, becoming sustainable, thinking it through, inviting in the community, modeling just relationships, understanding interdependence, modeling people over profit, and making relationships the most important part of the work. Can you imagine how many people want to really be a part of that?

Fellowship of the Gospel

We have a remarkable fellowship of good news. In the connectional church, we have a group of people that in their essence believe in the forgiveness and grace of Jesus Christ, based in the love of an awesome God. Because of this, we believe in justice, fairness, kindness, and humility. What better space is there to wrestle with how we might use whatever gifts we've been granted for the transformation we must make to create a more caring and sustainable community? We cannot make these kinds of changes alone. We must take the time to develop deep levels of trust and care as the economy and culture shifts to become the world we know we need.

Worship and Scripture

What a gift scripture and worship are to our life together! We can talk about relationships in ways that the rest of the culture so often does not initiate but is thirsty for. We can emphasize love and the value of human life and community above profits, efficiency, and independence. This is the gospel message.

Property

Churches own many properties and they spew greenhouse gases produced by heating, cooling, non-organic ways of gardening and lawn care, and by inefficient windows, walls, and ceilings. Church activities create waste. That garbage will either go into an incinerator or a landfill, both of which send more greenhouse gases into the atmosphere. They affect nearby communities right away and spread to other communities as the atmosphere heats up. Imagine if every church determined that their properties would model the best of sustainable practices!

Money

The gospel demands that we think about our money. "It will be hard for a rich person to enter the kingdom of heaven" (Matthew 9:23). So, where do we spend our money? Where do we save it? Where do we invest it? Money coupled with the gospel message must mean something! If we all worked at it, could we use our money to transform a wasteful, energy-obsessed economy? As a nation? As a community? As churches? As families? As individuals? The money that is in existence now has been earned from this unjust, unsustainable paradigm where those who have

money have somehow gotten the most from the least and where some continue to bear disproportionate effects of a system gone awry. What would it mean for all of us together to determine a new way?

Another Gift in the Church and in the World: Possible New Guides

We have recognized in The United Methodist Church that the church needs to repent of its actions toward indigenous peoples and needs to recognize the deep sense of indigenous spirituality that the church attempted to annihilate. Despite the many actions of the church that sought to erase indigenous peoples' cultures, some have maintained this deep sense of spirituality, of interdependence and love and care for the world they knew sustained them. Some indigenous peoples who have been able to stay on their land (though the quantity of land has dwindled) have been talking for generations about the ways the colonial/industrial way of "development" is unsustainable. Through incredibly powerful resilience and ecological understandings, some have taken care of many of our remaining forests and biodiversities, even as they've been exiled from decision-making circles.

As United Methodists we have stated the need to care for these relationships in Resolution 3334, "Native American Representation in The United Methodist Church" in *The Book of Resolutions of The United Methodist Church, 2012*:

> We will honor as sacred those practices that: call us back to the sacredness of Native people; affirm as beautiful their identity among the world's peoples; lead into right relationship with our Creator, creation and those around us; and call us into holy living. We call upon the world, the church, The United Methodist Church, and the people of The United Methodist Church to receive the gifts of Native people as people of God.[4]

The Baka Pygmies in Africa, for example, had understood for centuries, the vulnerable places of a forest and had elaborate spiritual rules, which protected these spaces. Watershed areas, catchment areas, and places where fragile ecosystems existed were thought to be filled with spirits, thus extra care was required. Ethics were taught through telling sacred stories. For instance, the Baka Pygmies were not to hunt during times when animals were reproducing, thus guaranteeing that the young animals would grow and thrive and mother animals would be able to nurse their young without intrusion. Another rule was that easily captured species were only to be hunted by persons who were initiated and elderly. Also, the consumption of some species was simply prohibited.[5] Those included the animals that often warned the Bakas that danger was on its way.

Yet, the Baka Pygmies have been denied access to their ancestral lands and the deep traditions that could help those of us who have been so integrated into the industrial development model understand ourselves and our sacred relationship to the natural world in more powerful ways.

According to Tebtebba, an organization that researches and advocates for indigenous peoples' rights, indigenous peoples have contributed to slowing climate change through their reverence for the forest and their sustainability practices. Yet, they have received little acknowledgement of their role or respect.

> Indigenous peoples have contributed much in preserving the forest massifs that are currently valued for their carbon sequestration role. But contemporary approaches to conservation have divested them of tenure and access rights, eschewed them from decision making, and dissuaded them from participating effectively in conservation programs that are proposed to them. . . . Baka traditional authority is not . . . recognized and their perception of the forest has been distorted with no means to protect their sacred groves from being depleted and destroyed by external stakeholders.[6]

As a people who for so many thousands of years were aware of their interdependence with the health and rejuvenation of the natural environment, even after all these years of marginalization, exploitation, and abuse, many strong enduring cultures of original peoples still have the gifts the rest of us need to bring the world back from the brink of disaster.

Other economically marginalized people groups have not only disproportionately experienced unjust effects of an unjust economic order, but are also the ones who endure the worst effects of climate change. One look at Haiti after Hurricane Sandy in 2012, which struck while the people were still recovering from the 2010 earthquake, or the Philippines after Typhoon Haiyan in 2013, or New Orleans after Hurricane Katrina in 2005, or the more impoverished areas of Brooklyn after Hurricane Sandy in 2012, would convince anyone that the people seriously affected by climate disasters are those on the economic and social margins. In the United States, people of color are disproportionately affected and around the world the impoverished elderly and young are the first to suffer and die. Seventy percent of the world's poor are women. Riveted by their circumstances and every breath they take, the industries in their neighborhoods and the zoning boards that turn their neighborhoods into sacrifice zones or put landfills in their back yards, some put everything they have into organizing for change. Building economic cooperatives where sustainable agricultural practices are the key or urban farms with important carbon-sequestering practices, or organizing against coal-fired power plants—one of the most egregious greenhouse gas emitters—these community activists have remarkable analysis, and environmental, agricultural, and political organizing knowledge to share with those who have benefited economically from industrial history.

Women are the world's household energy managers; they are on the forefront of what the family needs and why they need it—women make big decisions about the end products of an energy-intensive manufacturing process. Yet, in most conversations about energy, women are largely excluded. As United Methodist Women members, we need to consider this question: Wouldn't it be good if women were at the center of what works and what doesn't as we make the transformation?

Advocating for a New World

In a time when we suffer the consequences of our unjust, unsustainable, industrialized system, we must build a transformative economy. The growing inequity of political, economic, and social power is radically unsustainable. Working with our governments that control our infrastructure and encouraging action along the path of transformation is imperative.

The following principles can guide our government officials as they enact cultural and economic transformation.

- The best, most ecologically sound practices must be introduced system wide as central to our survival.
- Decision-making tables must be inclusive and responsive. Those who have suffered at the hands of a system they are ready to transform must be at the table. This will mean that power changes as we narrow the decision-making gap and resultant resource management and priorities.
- Social protection floors, protecting access to essential healthcare and basic income security, are important in this transition. Those who are most affected by the transformation (e.g. coal miners) and least able to cope with it must be supported in this time of transition.
- Sustainable, renewable energy industries must be encouraged. This means changing which industries are subsidized and paying attention to those who are laid off or in need of retraining, and how to put those people back to work.

United Methodist Women's Carbon Fund

Climate change is not an equal opportunity phenomenon.

Women and girls are on the frontlines of coping with the impact of climate change because of their economic status and the particular roles they play in society. They are also on the frontlines of creating alternative strategies and solutions. In developing countries, women and girls often are responsible for the most basic survival needs of their families, water, fuel, and food. When these become more costly or scarce, women and girls' work increases. At the grassroots level, women are often well positioned to manage risk due to their roles as both users and managers of environmental resources, as economic providers, and as caregivers and community workers.

Most policymakers and development workers do not take gender roles into account or incorporate women's voices. Therefore, their efforts to halt climate change and help communities adapt often exacerbate existing gender inequalities and are not as effective as they need to be.

This is why United Methodist Women created a Women's Carbon Fund. As such, the carbon fund will be guided by United Methodist Women and used to create solidarity with initiatives that seek to make a difference in the carbon economy. More information is on the United Methodist Women website: **www.unitedmethodist women.org/carbonfund.**

- Provision for those who suffer immediate loss of health, housing, food, or displacement caused by climate change. They must be cared for and restored to full and voiced influence.
- Industries need to be held responsible for their reticence to change.
- The reeducation of workforce and workforce management is necessary so that the move from an industrialized economy to one that works at sustainable, green cooperative, reuseable, recyclable production, and just distribution of profits can take place.
- The economy based upon a waste production cycle needs to change to cradle-to-cradle production cycles. Cradle-to-cradle production means that those who produce do not just make something but take responsibility for its production, use, and byproducts. Additionally, it means to reuse and create secondary products from the primary ones. This type of production ensures that those responsible for the production are also responsible for its waste and thus are incentivized to reuse and recycle.

International Advocacy

Climate change and the mechanisms that create it and result from it are ripe with historical and current inequities. As the church, this understanding needs to form the foundation of our work together, even when addressing international understandings. A U.S.-centric patriotism without an understanding of the experiences of neighbors in another country is not gospel behavior.

Although each one of us needs to be a part of the solution, not all peoples and nations have inherited the same resources, and many have not benefited from industrialization in the same way. Women, the impoverished, migrants, small family farmers, and indigenous peoples all have and will continue to bear disproportionate effects of climate change. Those nations and peoples who have profited from the last 180 years of greenhouse gas-producing industrialized development need to take greater responsibility for the concerns that are before us.

The Conference of Parties (COP) of the United Nations Framework Convention on Climate Change (UNFCCC), which meets every fall, has been stuck for many sessions as the world has watched. The problem? Large gross domestic product (GDP) carbon-emitting countries have blocked progress over the concerns brought to the floor by nations that do not have a large GDP at all. Those countries, which emit fewer greenhouse gases, have asked that the convention enumerate "common but differentiated responsibilities" around climate change and disasters. The Philippines for two years in a row (2012 and 2013) came to the COP immediately after experiencing horrendous typhoons. Each year with a hushed crowd around them, they spoke from a place of authority born through such suffering. Climate change has a disproportionate effect on those who have contributed little to create it. The Philippines urgently pled with the COP of the UNFCCC to make the decisions it needed to reduce greenhouse gas emissions in a dramatic way. Representatives from Tuvalu, Kripalu, and other small Pacific islands spoke of being threatened with annihilation—their peoples and cultures relegated to a new climate diaspora—as climate refugees. The poorest areas of the world have populations whose livelihoods have been supported by indigenous knowledge of the land, air, and water—whose small farms keep their families alive—already know that climate change must be urgently addressed, yet they have a small voice in these large conferences that determine their fate.

In 2014, Secretary of State John Kerry indicated the willingness of the United States to more urgently negotiate when he told the Indonesian people that climate change could be considered the new terrorist. Together, he said, we needed to move ahead in more powerful ways.[7] He did not, however, take an account of our common but differentiated responsibilities. This is the stickler.

- We need to advocate that the U.S. government take seriously its historic role in the industrialized economic system's global reach, our much higher gross national product (GNP), and how this fosters and exacerbates inequalities among nations and peoples.

- We need to acknowledge that those who have profited more from this industrial economy must bear greater responsibility than those who have not; both national and global taxation systems must be used to transform our economic relationships.

Special Attention

One of the most insidious complexities we face is the necessity to move from fossil fuels and their greenhouse gas emissions to sustainable forms of energy and lifestyles *while* ensuring that those who have so little access to energy and/or resources are able to access them. One in five people worldwide still lack access to modern energy. Three billion people rely on wood, coal, charcoal, or animal waste for cooking and heating; burning these is carbon intensive. Yet, cheap forms of energy such as coal or other high carbon dioxide–emitting forms of energy such as the tar sands in Alberta, Canada, aren't the solution. Right now, energy is the dominant contributor to climate change.[8] Reducing carbon-emitting energy sources must be a universal priority. What does this mean for our churches? What might we do to ensure that our churches are not taking more than their fair share and modeling a new energy consciousness for the sake of those who have no modern energy sources?

About Us: Caretakers of God's Creation

"Caretakers of God's Creation is a grassroots community of United Methodists who believe that a relationship with God's creation and a ministry of caring for and healing the earth are integral to what it means to be a Christian. Both Christian scripture and Wesleyan theology are central to our belief that the earth belongs to God, not us, and we are given the responsibility to be good stewards of it. Our mission is to be a transformative Christian witness, helping others to know God as revealed through creation and motivating them to act on behalf of environmental wholeness and justice.

"The United Methodist Church is a global church, at work in approximately 130 countries around the world with 8 million members. Given the global nature of the environmental problems the earth faces and the strength of our numbers, we have faith that we will make a significant difference in the world.

"In order to accomplish our task, we will raise the level of theological understanding among our members, we will encourage, by example, joyful stewardship through sustainable living, and we will advocate for public policy engagement on local, state, national, and international levels."[9]

Right now, the industrial, extractive model of development is grabbing land, resources, and business deals around the world, which those who are supportive of this way of development say will increase the GDP of many poorer countries. Yet, the beneficiaries of this kind of land, resource, and business model are rarely the poorest among us; one could make a point to say that it's not benefiting those who have little access to energy. In fact, land grabbing, resource extraction, and its resulting environmental degradation usually make many people even poorer as their ability to farm and find water diminishes. And all of this grabbing emits more greenhouse gases and toxic waste.

Because fossil fuels are pervasive and affect each aspect of our extraction, production, and waste cycles, they are key factors to climate change and its devastating consequences. Let's begin to seriously redefine the good life. The biblical definition of the good life is a place to start for that revisioning.

Integrity and Personal and Organizational Transformation

It's interesting to me when we become incensed over the carbon emissions of a power plant or the placement of a landfill or even rail against pollution during a church education hour, but fail to reduce our own waste, turn the air conditioning on full blast, or do not recognize the connections between pollution and racial justice. Our actions encourage those power plants to produce more and more, and affirm the need for that large landfill. We make others suffer because of our own lack of care. What can we do ourselves? What more can we do as a church, as United Methodist Women members?

Reduce consumption. To lessen greenhouse gas emissions, those of us who overconsume must reduce our consumption. This is simplistic on one level and deeply convicting on another. We cannot just reduce our consumption; we must also care about what that does to the workers who produce what we consume. The jobs they hold now, however unlivable their salaries may be, are a lifeline. Thus, we must couple this reduction in our consumption with investment in sustainable practices, regulations, transformative processes, and reeducation of workforces to those things that reduce energy use and help

Some Energy Alternatives

In Oaxaca, Mexico, European corporations are hungrily eyeing the Isthmus of Tehuantepec for development of large-scale wind farms. However, indigenous peoples live in the area and most of the energy companies that have come in have marginalized these communities by disrespecting legal obligations to them and failing to provide adequate information. It was into this context that Yansa was born. Yansa, named after the goddess of wind, is a cooperatively owned wind energy farm whose proceeds directly support the community. This citizen-owned sustainable energy source needs to be the model for reducing energy poverty.

After seeing the movie *An Inconvenient Truth*, two young teens in Washington, D.C., asked their parents to go solar. The parents began to research and talk with companies, but they found solar too expensive and confusing. They told their children, "If we're going to do this, we need the whole neighborhood to go solar," thinking that would be the end of it. But the teens made and delivered fliers asking if their neighbors wanted to join the Mt. Pleasant Solar Co-op meeting. Fifty people came to that meeting, and from there they formed a movement that has gone citywide. In 2008, they passed a bill through the city council that created long-term solar power incentives for the District of Columbia. It was important to the founders of DC Solar that solar energy would be affordable and accessible to anyone who wanted to go solar. Today, there is a co-op in each of Washington D.C.'s eight wards.[10]

us more powerfully reduce, reuse, and recycle. Then, the jobs would shift. NAACP's climate justice program has completed a study called "Just Energy Policies: Reducing Pollution and Creating Jobs" that explores what would happen if we shifted to almost 100 percent renewable energy sources and, at the same time, care for jobs lost by those who currently work in extraction, production, and waste.[11] We need to understand the need for government-financed social safety nets and the important way the government and others can participate in support of and reeducation of the workforce as this transition takes place.

Take care of and recycle almost everything. Though recycling still takes energy and emits greenhouse gases, it is much better than throwing items into a landfill or burning them in an incinerator, and definitely better than backyard barrel burning! This is a value we need to instill in those of us who grew up in the postwar baby boom. We have become a throw-away generation. Industry thrives on our buying the next great thing. Cradle-to-cradle manufacturing and production will help a new ethic take the place of consumerism and convenience.

Reuse as much as we can. Adapting from the use of raw materials to reusing them over and over again is a powerful and important creative process that will inherently affect the economic system! It is for this reason that we must focus on the need for governmental safety nets and the imperative provision for the reeducation of the workforce.

Conclusion

For the sake of John's vision of a tree of life over the crystal river and the healing of the nations, the church must take action.

- We need to take up the mantle and become the healer between the church and the earth. Our vision and theology can reenvision ourselves as the tree of life whose fruit never ends by the crystal waters. We can take actions that are real with tangible results, and this can happen in the church.
- The church needs to be the bridge between those who are rich and those who are impoverished. We must actively seek out relationships with those on "the other side" and work to ensure that those relationships lead to more justice. This will require advocating for taxation and social security systems, solidarity with those at the bottom of the economy, and increased understanding of the deep need we have to build an economy that decreases the divide. We need to do this, as climate change continues to wreak

No Plastic… Save the Environment Through Alternatives project was organized by the Centre for Action and Rural Education in Erode, Tamil Nadu, India, and supported by United Methodist Women. *Photo credit: CARE, India*

havoc. These efforts can happen throughout the church.

- We need to understand what it is to have interdependent relationships with one another—where those throughout the United States or across the sea are experienced as intimately linked with us. This education can occur in the church.
- We need to set up tables where those at the heart of political power sit down with the most marginalized and figure out together what we can do so that all can have access to the things that make for life, and no one can have more than what is good for the ecology around them. This can begin in the church.
- We need to heal the rifts and announce the good news to the earth and its people so that the church becomes the tree under which we all might find not only relief, but also justice for those who have experienced such vast injustice.
- We need to have a vision for a common world where there are differentiated responsibilities because of the inequity of the present economic order.

- We need to support women as energy managers, and the most marginalized communities moving to the center as the key transformation we need to make.

When and if the church becomes the voice in the wilderness with this vision and focused action in its heart and hands, it will be a tree of life bearing fruit, yielding fruit every month, whose leaves will heal peoples and the nations. Thank God. ✪

Endnotes

1. William Wordsworth, "The World is too much with Us" *Poems, In Two Volumes*, 1807.

2. "Mission & Vision," Kentuckians for the Commonwealth, accessed March 31, 2014, www.kftc.org/about-us/mission-vision.

3. "About the Evergreen Cooperatives," Evergreen Cooperatives, accessed March 20, 2014, http://evergreencooperatives.com/about.

4. "Native American Representation in The United Methodist Church," Resolution 3334, *The Book of Resolutions of The United Methodist Church* (Nashville: Abingdon Press, 2012).

5. "Indigenous Peoples, Forests and REDD Plus: Sustaining and Enhancing Forests Through Traditional Resource Management," volume 2 (Baguio City, Philippines: Tebtebba Foundation, 2013), 33–39.

6. Ibid., 66.

7. John Kerry, "Remarks on Climate Change," U.S. Department of State, February 16, 2014, www.state.gov/secretary/remarks/2014/02/221704.htm.

8. "Sustainable Energy for All," The Future We Want, United Nations, accessed March 21, 2014, www.un.org/en/sustainablefuture/energy.asp.

9. "About Us," Caretakers of God's Creation, accessed March 20, 2014, www.umccreationcare.org/#!about_us/csgz.

10. "Tell the PSC to reject the Exelon-Pepco merger," DC Sun, accessed March 20, 2014, www.dcsun.org, and Joan Shipps, "How Grassroots Activists in D.C. Are Taking on a Corporate Titan—And Winning," *The Huffington Post*, April 13, 2015, www.huffingtonpost.com/joan-shipps/how-grassroots-activists-_b_7034086.html.

11. "Just Energy Policies: Reducing Pollution and Creating Jobs," National Association for the Advancement of Colored People (NAACP) Environmental and Climate Justice Program, December 2013, accessed April 7, 2014, http://naacp.3cdn.net/8654c676dbfc968f8f_dk7m6j5v0.pdf.

About the Author

The Reverend Kathleen Stone is an ordained elder in The United Methodist Church who currently serves in the United Methodist Women Office of Environmental and Economic Justice. Previously, she served as chaplain of the Church Center for the United Nations, as program director for the General Board of Church and Society's United Nations Ministry, and has served both as associate pastor and senior pastor in local churches in the Greater New Jersey Annual Conference. She is a proud mom to two grown sons.

United Methodist Women from around the country joined a host of United Methodists—and about 400,000 others—in the People's Climate March, a historic climate justice event in New York City in September 2014. *Photo by Andrew Cheu*

Chapter 8

Climate Justice: How Can We Make It Happen?

Sharon Delgado

As we read and assimilate the materials from this study on climate justice, we need to consider how we will apply what we are learning. The goal of this chapter is to help equip participants to join or establish creation care ministry teams in their annual conferences to create a network that is strong enough to transform the church and the world. Creation care ministry teams provide a context in which we can work together through The United Methodist Church and beyond to create a cultural shift and to transform the system that is causing climate change.

How can we rise to the occasion, discern a healing path, and help lead the way into a future of justice for the most vulnerable among us, future generations, and all creation? The challenges before us are many. The transition to a world of climate justice will require a huge cultural shift, extending into the world's political and economic systems. It will take a reordering of values, priorities, and public policies at every decision-making level.

Fortunately, we are not alone in this work. God is present and the Spirit is actively at work in the redemption of the world even today. Jesus said, "The Son can do nothing on his own, but only what he sees the Father doing; for whatever the Father does, the Son does likewise" (John 5:19b). Jesus discerned God's activity and moved in the direction that he saw God working. As followers of Jesus, we are called and empowered to do

the same. "For it is God who is at work in you, enabling you both to will and work for [God's] good pleasure" (Philippians 2:13).

As United Methodists and as followers of Jesus, God is working in us and through us. Certainly it is "God's good pleasure" for our poor and vulnerable brothers and sisters throughout the world to be lifted up, for blessings to abound to future generations, and for compassion to be extended to all parts of creation. Surely God will help us discern a path, give us the tools we need, and empower us to be leaders in moving our churches to become a powerful force in the healing of creation. As we accept our calling, commit ourselves to climate justice, and step into leadership, we can trust that God is working through us to bring transformation and healing to the world.

Creating a Cultural Shift

Creating a cultural shift involves a widespread transformation of attitudes, values, and lifestyles. This is no small task, but our churches are uniquely situated to help bring this about. Our bishops have spoken on these issues. Our General Conference has spoken out over the years, and will continue to speak. Their statements are prophetic and clear. Our challenge is to translate these statements into action and bring them to life.

We can begin by taking the first steps on this journey into leadership in our own local units of

United Methodist Women, in our own congregations, and in our own annual conferences. We can begin to form creation care ministry teams by inviting people to join together for prayer, study, and action on the issues of climate justice, with the help of this book or other denominational resources. In this way, we begin the process of changing attitudes, values, and lifestyles in our churches and contribute to the cultural shift that is required.

Many local churches are becoming more "green," with concern for creation reflected in their worship, structures, maintenance, and ministries. Lawns are being transformed into community gardens, enabling congregations to join in the global movement toward sustainable agriculture, contribute to the community, and participate in an economy of sharing. Energy audits of church facilities are resulting in the installation of energy-efficient appliances, LED lighting, and in some cases, solar panels. Some churches incorporate prayers for the earth into worship and many churches organize an annual Earth Day Sunday service. These and other creation care ministries provide a model of faithfulness for congregational members and a witness to the larger community of Christian concern for the earth.

As leaders seeking to incorporate creation justice into every aspect of theology and mission, we can build on this movement to "green" the church. As we do so, it is important to nurture hope within others and ourselves. This hope is not optimism. When looking at scientific projections and the plight of current victims of climate change, we could easily become pessimistic. Hope is not built upon probable outcomes, but upon faith that the God who brought creation into being is active still and can work through us to bring about a future that we cannot yet see.

One way to nurture hope is to join with others who are similarly committed to climate justice. Not only can members of a small group of like-minded people encourage each other, even a small group of two or three can provide leaven that can raise awareness in local units of United Methodist Women and among congregation members.

The United Methodist Church offers openness to a diversity of perspectives on theology and on social and environmental issues. This flexibility can provide a forum within our churches for loving and thoughtful dialogue on these issues.

Nevertheless, working to raise congregational awareness about climate justice, or about any contemporary issue, can be extremely challenging. Our church home, where we are spiritually nurtured, may be the last place we want to raise an issue that could create controversy or discord among members. Still, our churches will need to wrestle with these issues if we are to live into the future that God intends. As climate justice leaders, we can look to the prophets and to Jesus as we call our congregations to join in this work, for the sake of our human family, especially the most vulnerable, for the sake of future generations, and for the sake of the whole creation.

Of course, it is helpful if the pastor and other congregational leaders are supportive of such efforts, but they may also need to be educated about climate justice. Few seminaries teach courses on these subjects. Some church leaders may be resistant. Still, study groups can form around denominational resources, and actions can be taken by United Methodist Women groups or by other small groups within the church.

It can be encouraging to join with groups beyond the local church that are engaged in working for a just and ecologically sustainable world. Forming connections with such groups can be mutually supportive and can multiply our efforts. Connecting with members of other faith communities can stimulate interfaith dialogue and action that can impact the wider community, and can provide a model of cooperation that will be necessary as we move toward a world of climate justice. Likewise, working with secular groups focused on peace, justice, and environmental issues can broaden our perspective and illumine the breadth and diversity of the cultural shift that is already taking place, in spite of the many forces that are working to maintain the status quo.

Creation care leaders can also find support by reaching out to other United Methodists in their annual conferences and throughout the United Methodist connection. Creation care ministry teams will enable us to encourage each other and multiply our impact on the United Methodist Church and on the world.

The United Methodist Church has long acknowledged the reality of climate change and has, from the beginning, linked environmental concerns with concern for poor and impoverished people around the world. We can draw from our denomination's expertise and experience and use its resources and tools in order to educate others and ourselves for action on these issues. As we do so, we will find encouragement, support, and hope as we journey together in the direction of "God's good pleasure" for creation.

Resources for Ministry and Mission

Our work to transform our churches must extend beyond our church buildings into the realms of ministry and mission. This will require a new theology of the mission of the church, a theology that takes seriously the integration of creation care, justice, and active participation in the work of healing and transforming the world.

General Board of Discipleship

Church ministries can incorporate these essentials at every level of service, including worship. A statement from the General Board of Discipleship (GBOD) addresses climate change and worship, pointing out that not many congregations pray for the earth and its creatures, our baptismal vows do not directly challenge us to care for the earth, and The United Methodist Church does not have a specific agency charged with helping us live out our calling as stewards of the earth.[1]

GBOD proposes several remedies. First, the board challenges us to "add the earth and all God's creatures to your prayer list this Sunday, and keep them there!"[2] Second, although adding a commitment to care for the earth as part of the official baptismal ritual requires General Conference action, meanwhile we can teach that "resisting evil, injustice, and oppression in whatever forms they present themselves" includes resisting forces that destroy human life or disrupt the earth's ecosystems.[3] Finally, GBOD challenges us to reduce the carbon emissions we emit in the places where we worship and in our transportation to and from worship. As we worship God, we are called to witness to God's love for all creation.

Other ministries can also incorporate the awareness of climate justice. Children's ministries can integrate love of creation and care for the poor, including people in distant lands. Ministries with youth can provide a forum for young people to consider what it means to be responsible members of the community of life, to struggle with the great social and environmental issues of our day, and to listen for God's call. Adult education ministries can engage the many denominational resources that are available, including resources made available by United Methodist Women.

United Methodist Women

United Methodist Women has been a leader in the movement to "green" The United Methodist Church, and continues to be. The organization, with its focus on mission to women, children, and youth, has been especially active in environmental justice ministries. Today, climate justice is one of its four social justice priorities. United Methodist Women offers study materials, programs and campaigns, and other resources for ministries that address interrelated forms of injustice, including injustice based on gender and race, economic injustice, and climate injustice.

Many practical resources are available on the United Methodist Women's Climate Change and Environmental Justice web page.[4] The "13 Steps to Sustainability" provides a list of thirteen practical ways to gather for church events in ways that reduce environmental harm, foster just relationships, and raise awareness of God's call to creation care. The tagline of this initiative is "Be Just. Be Green." This phrase is an apt summary of the call to climate justice, expressing the truth that justice and environmental sustainability belong together.

When organizing an event, choose and follow through with one or more of these thirteen guidelines. At the next gathering, add another. The point is not to be perfect, but to enter into the sometimes-difficult process of transformation. As we shift our understanding, awareness, and practices, we become part of the cultural shift that we want to see in the world.

The United Methodist Women's Climate Change and Environmental Justice web page also provides links to helpful tools, including the Environmental Protection Agency's carbon footprint calculator, which enables individuals to discover how much they contribute to climate change. A related resource is offered by the nonprofit Interfaith Power and Light, which offers a Cool Congregations Calculator to measure the carbon footprints of congregations and suggests ways to reduce them.[5] This sobering process can help us break out of denial and begin to take responsibility for our part in contributing to the carbon pollution that leads to climate change.

The concept of "carbon footprint" can provide a jumping-off point for a focus on climate justice. United Methodist Women, congregations, or annual conference members can calculate their own carbon footprints and support each other in finding ways to reduce them. This process of reducing our carbon footprints is one step we can take in the process of reducing harm and creating a cultural shift. As we do this, we join in solidarity with the victims of the profligate use of fossil fuels and with others who are seeking climate justice. At the same time, we practice integrity as our words that proclaim climate justice are embodied by our actions.

Some groups promote "carbon offsets" as a way to make up for carbon emissions by investing in tree planting, solar development, methane disposal, and other projects. The motto of Carbonfund.org is "reduce what you can, offset what you can't."[6] The concept of offsetting carbon pollution is controversial, however. Some argue that carbon offsets offer a loophole to the more difficult work of changing lifestyles and corporate practices; they may work to assuage consciences and appease regulators, but help to perpetuate the overall problem. Some point out that the system of offsetting carbon emissions can be gamed, that many of these projects might have gone forward anyway, and that there is no guarantee that projects approved for offset credits actually reduce overall emissions.[7] Creation ministry teams may want to study the issue of carbon offsets as part of the process of reducing carbon emissions as individuals and as a group.

Whether you support carbon offsets or not, it is valuable to contribute financially to the work of climate justice. The Women's Carbon Fund, created by United Methodist Women, is one way to do so. Highlighting this fund can help raise awareness about climate justice while contributing practically to efforts to bring it about. The Women's Carbon Fund supports projects led by women that lower carbon emissions; projects led by women that help women, families, and communities that are affected by climate change adapt to new conditions; and advocacy initiatives that are led by women for women, and that seek equitable and sustainable solutions related to climate and energy. Information about this fund is available on the United Methodist Women's Climate Change and Environmental Justice web page.[8]

General Board of Global Ministries

In January 2014, the General Board of Global Ministries established a global missionary role dedicated to the care of God's creation. There are four main tasks of this position:

1. Expand Caretakers of God's Creation, a creation care ministry of the Virginia Conference, to a national level that encourages all annual conferences to implement their own creation care ministry teams and to equip them with resources to help empower them to do their work.

2. Assess global mission programs and projects to ascertain what we're already doing to care for God's creation and to strengthen those ministries, and to identify areas that may be harmful to the environment and suggest changes to those programs.

3. Work with the United Methodist Council of Bishops based on their 2009 document, "God's Renewed Creation" on ways in which that document can be better integrated into the life of the church.

4. Write an Environmental Policy Statement and accompanying Implementation Manual for measuring the environmental footprint of how Global Ministries does its work in our offices in New York, Atlanta, and the regional offices in Africa, Latin America, and Asia.

Our Bishops Speak

In 2009 the United Methodist Council of Bishops released "God's Renewed Creation: Call to Hope and Action," a pastoral letter that addresses three interrelated threats to life and hope: pandemic poverty and disease, environmental degradation, and the proliferation of weapons and violence. The Call to Hope and Action website[9] includes a slideshow[10] and other practical resources that can help creation care ministry teams raise these issues in settings of worship and study, interpret them theologically, and prepare for faithful action. The pastoral letter can be printed in newsletters, read aloud in worship, educational gatherings, or other events. The foundation document presents an in-depth background on these issues that affect God's creation. The Guide for Group Study can be used with older youth and adults, and the Guide for Teachers of Children offers ways that children can be taught to care for creation.

"Call to Hope and Action" is an invitation from the United Methodist bishops to join them in working for transformation as stewards of God's creation. Our bishops remind us that it is God who is working through us as we seek to bring healing to the world: "Despite these interconnected threats to life and hope, God's creative work continues. Despite the ways we all contribute to these problems, God still invites each one of us to participate in the work of renewal. We must begin the work of renewing creation by being renewed in our own hearts and minds. We cannot help the world until we change our way of being in it."[11]

General Board of Church and Society

The General Board of Church and Society (GBCS) educates and advocates for climate justice from a faith perspective throughout the denomination, in its interfaith work, in governments, and in international settings. GBCS attends United

Nations climate summits while working with regional churches wherever those summits are held. In 2011, GBCS brought together young adults from across Africa to form a delegation to the United Nations climate conference in Durban, South Africa. In 2014, at the UN climate conference in Lima, Peru, the GBCS participated closely with leaders of the Methodist Church of Peru.[12]

Creation care ministry leaders will discover a wealth of practical resources from GBCS. Updated information about The United Methodist Church's work for climate justice can be found by searching GBCS's website with the search terms "global warming and energy."[13]

A primary way that GBCS works on issues of environmental and climate justice is through building networks and coordinating actions in collaboration with ecumenical and interfaith allies. The board works closely with Creation Justice Ministries, which represent the creation care and environmental justice policies of major Christian denominations throughout the United States, including The United Methodist Church, and works cooperatively with many other faith bodies. Creation Justice Ministries' website includes many resources for climate justice, including study guides, campaign information, and stories from around the church. The organization develops Earth Day materials each year to help congregations celebrate and care for God's creation. Its website proclaims, "Justice for God's Planet and God's people."[14]

United Methodist Committee on Relief

The wealthier nations, particularly the United States, are responsible for most of the greenhouse gas emissions that are now causing climate change. Poor nations, and poor people within nations, are less able to mitigate and adapt to rising temperatures, rising sea levels, and extreme weather events.

Many people in island nations, Africa (home to some of the poorest countries in the world), indigenous communities, and other nations that have contributed little to climate pollution, are already experiencing its harmful effects. Small, low-lying islands are especially vulnerable to disastrous flooding in the event of tidal waves, hurricanes, monsoon, or other serious storms.

The United Methodist Committee on Relief (UMCOR) is beginning to address the impacts of climate change in its responses to weather-related disasters. An April 2014 article by Susan Kerr, published on UMCOR's website, proclaims, "Climate Change Has Become a Disaster." The article points out that disasters are worsened by warmer ocean temperatures and rising seas.[15] UMCOR has held a series of trainings geared toward assisting island nations to prepare for disasters brought about by climate change.[16]

Climate scientists tell us that if greenhouse gas emissions continue unabated, the number of extreme weather events will multiply, leading to more disasters and more suffering. We must respond to the calls for climate justice from the many communities and nations that are being harmed even now. Our mission projects must continue to offer relief but must also incorporate the long-term work of mitigating greenhouse gas emissions and helping communities and countries adapt to the damaging impacts of climate change.

General Board of Pensions and Health Benefits

The General Board of Pensions and Health Benefits (GBPHB) works on issues of climate change in an advisory and advocacy capacity with companies in their portfolio. Many of these companies, including Exxon Mobile, Conoco Phillips, and Occidental Petroleum, contribute directly to global warming through greenhouse gas emissions.

GBPHB points out that all companies are susceptible to the effects of climate change, and advises the companies it invests in to consider future financial opportunities and risks to shareholders posed by climate change. The board also encourages companies to voluntarily report on their response to issues relating to climate change. In January 2015, GBPHB announced that it will establish an investment screen on thermal coal. Some United Methodists are calling on GBPHB to take stronger action on climate change by divesting from the production of fossil fuels altogether.

This approach may seem extreme, but major institutional changes will be required to bring about a world of climate justice. The culture is shifting as people adopt simpler and more environmentally friendly lifestyles. Many people are reducing and offsetting their carbon footprints. Yet the overall burning of fossil fuels and emissions of greenhouse gases continue to accelerate. According to the Intergovernmental Panel on Climate Change, in the first decade of the twenty-first century greenhouse gas emissions grew at a rate almost double that of the previous thirty years.[17] The current global system is unsustainable. As leaders in creation care ministries, our challenge will include working to change the system that is creating climate change.

System Change, Not Climate Change

As leaders of creation care ministries, it is important to educate others and ourselves about the institutional and systemic pressures that block strong government action toward climate justice. Climate change is an unintended consequence of a global system that produces vast wealth and leaves poverty, inequity, conflict, and environmental devastation in its wake. Even as people around the world cry out for change, today's global system of advanced free market capitalism continues to gain momentum, supported by political, economic, and military power.

The U.S. political process is itself dominated by wealth and corporate power. Policy makers,

beholden to corporate sponsors, approve huge subsidies for large corporations. Some of the largest subsidies and tax breaks go to the fossil fuels industry. These oil, gas, and coal corporations degrade the earth and pollute the atmosphere with greenhouse gases through methods that include hydraulic fracturing (fracking), mountaintop removal, offshore oil drilling, and the mining of tar sands and other forms of unconventional, or so-called dirty fuels. At the same time, they spend millions to support the candidates of their choice, lobby against climate legislation, and fund climate change denial. If we stay on the current course, greenhouse gas emissions will continue to accelerate and we will face runaway climate change.

These are the realities behind the movement to divest from fossil fuels. The "Go Fossil Free" divestment campaign was started by Bill McKibben, an author, climate activist, and United Methodist Sunday school teacher. The gofossilfree.org website states: "If it is wrong to wreck the climate, then it is wrong to profit from that wreckage. We believe that educational and religious institutions, city and state governments, and other institutions that serve the public good should divest from fossil fuels."[18]

Fossil Free UMC is a network of concerned United Methodists that extends across the denomination, with coordinated activity in several annual conferences. This coalition has been working on legislation to be voted on at the 2016 General Conference. If passed, a screen against companies that produce fossil fuels would be added to current investment screens based on United Methodist Social Principles. Current investment screens include those that directly or indirectly, "support racial discrimination, violation of human rights, sweatshop or forced labor, gambling, or the production of nuclear armaments, alcoholic beverages or tobacco, or companies dealing in pornography."[19]

If we are committed to the vision of a peaceful, just, and environmentally sustainable world, we will have to change the way we do business, both in the church and in society as a whole. We will have to change not only our lifestyles, but also our social, technological, economic, and political institutions. The current system is not designed to further human well-being, protect natural or cultural resources, or protect the gifts of creation. That's why signs at demonstrations say, "System change, not climate change." McKibben said, "You . . . need to do more than change your light bulbs. You need to try to change the system that is raising the temperature, the sea level, the extinction rate—even raising the question of how well civilization will survive this century."[20]

International Negotiations

Climate change is a global problem, and will take global cooperation to resolve. The nations of the world have been meeting regularly for climate summits since 1992, yet we are still far from an effective international treaty.

Issues of climate justice are front and center at these high-level meetings. In November 2013, leaders from more than 190 nations met in Warsaw, Poland, for UN climate negotiations. Typhoon Haiyan, the strongest storm ever to make landfall,[21] had hit the Philippines just days before. Yeb Sano, Filipino delegate at the summit, made an emotional appeal and fasted for the duration of the talks, calling on negotiators to take bold action on climate change. An interfaith group in Warsaw, which included United Methodists, joined him in fasting, as did many people around the world. [22]

On November 20, the tenth day of Yeb Sano's fast, developing nations walked out of the climate talks because of the refusal by wealthier nations to agree to a financial mechanism to address "loss and damage" caused by climate change. This protest highlighted the fact that fossil fuels emissions now causing climate change have mostly come from industrialized nations, especially the United States, while poor nations suffer the worst consequences.

People of the Philippines, African nations, the Maldives and other island nations, and other hard-hit countries are pleading with those of us in wealthier, more powerful nations to take climate negotiations seriously. Even as systemic inertia carries us forward on the current course toward climate disaster, we are called to be in solidarity with and to advocate for people who are most vulnerable and those who are already suffering the effects of climate change. Those of us who live in the global North must listen and respond to the voices of climate activists from the global South, women who live on the front lines of climate change, young people who speak out and take action for future generations, and indigenous peoples calling on us to respect the rights of the earth.[23]

The United Methodist Church, "supports efforts of all governments to require mandatory reductions in greenhouse gas emissions."[24] As creation care ministry leaders we can join the United Methodist Women and GBCS to advocate for a global treaty with binding limits on emissions and with mechanisms for wealthier nations to financially assist poor and vulnerable nations in adapting to the ravages of climate change. This will require those of us who are leaders to join in the chorus of voices calling for system change, not climate change.

Market-Based Solutions

Market-based mechanisms will need to be enforced if we are to transition away from a fossil fuels based economy. As long as oil, gas, and coal are cheaper than alternative sources of energy, transitioning away from fossil fuels will be difficult. One solution is to shift government subsidies from environmentally harmful to environmentally sustainable industries. We could

United Methodist Women members and about 400,000 others attended the People's Climate March, a historic climate justice event in New York City to impact a United Nations climate summit on September 23, 2014. *Photo by Andrew Cheu*

stop subsidizing the fossil fuels industry and shift all that money into investments in conservation and renewable energy. We could stop subsidizing corporate agribusiness, with its emphasis on fossil fuel–based fertilizers, pesticides, and genetic modification technologies and instead invest tax dollars in speeding up the cultural shift to organic and locally based agriculture. In this way some of the vast resources currently directed toward continuing harmful practices would be diverted into more just and environmentally friendly alternatives.

Another market-based approach is a fee and dividend system proposed by former NASA scientist James Hanson and supported by the advocacy group Citizens Climate Lobby.[25] This would involve putting a fee on carbon at the source of extraction (that is, at the mine, the oil

well, or fracking rig), or at the point of entry, but then disburse the proceeds equally to every man, woman, and child in the United States to offset the rising costs of fuel. Most people would get back as much or more money in dividends than they would pay in higher energy prices. This would foster both sustainability and justice by making it expensive for big polluters to pollute and by providing incentives for conservation at every income level, without disproportionately burdening working families or the poor.

These common sense market solutions may seem politically impossible at this time, because the fossil fuel industry has so much political power. That reality only strengthens the case that the system itself needs to change.

Building a Global Movement

How can we possibly transform the current global system, the most powerful system in the history of the world? Is such an all-encompassing transformation even possible? Can we hold fast to a vision of God's intended world even in this time of climate disruption and under threat of runaway climate change?

In a 2014 interview on Moyers and Company, Bill McKibben made the case for building a peoples' movement strong enough to transform the global system, prevent catastrophic climate change, and change the world. "Most people understand that we're in a serious fix," he said. "There's nothing you can do as individuals that will really slow down this juggernaut . . . You can say the same thing about the challenges faced by people in the civil rights or the abolition movement, or the gay rights movement or the women's movement. In each case, a movement arose; if we can build a movement, then we have a chance."[26]

Fortunately, there is a global movement for climate justice that is strong and growing. McKibben started 350.org, a worldwide organization that mobilizes people to challenge governments to reduce the levels of carbon dioxide in the atmosphere to below a sustainable 350 parts per million. Every year, thousands of groups on every continent organize themselves autonomously, but coordinate their actions with 350.org to raise awareness of the urgency of the climate crisis.[27]

The Climate Reality Project, headed by former Vice President Al Gore, trains people on every continent to give slideshows on the dangers of climate change. Their website has educational materials and information about their campaigns, such as "Reality Drop: Spread Truth, Destroy Denial."[28]

Climate Justice Now is a global coalition of groups working for "social, ecological, and gender justice." Their website has a wealth of information about what groups around the world are doing to influence societies and governments to create a more just and ecologically sustainable world.[29]

Interfaith Action

Faith-based organizations are educating and motivating members of faith communities to become part of the movement to prevent catastrophic climate change and to bring healing to the earth and the human community. There are countless ecumenical and interfaith organizations that focus on caring for creation and reducing the impacts of climate change, including Creation Justice Ministries, as mentioned above. Greenfaith, based in New Jersey,[30] and Earth Ministry, based in Washington State,[31] are two excellent examples of such ministries. Interfaith Power and Light (IPL) is an interfaith organization, with affiliates throughout the United States, that works with faith communities to educate members about climate change, to facilitate their shift to efficient and renewable power, and to model stewardship of God's creation. IPL also organizes congregations to advocate for energy policies that reduce greenhouse gas pollution, protect God's creation, and support impacted communities.[32]

The National Religious Partnership for the Environment has worked with various U.S. faith communities on environmental issues, including climate change, since the 1980s.[33] The World Council of Churches (WCC) brings together churches and denominations throughout the world, including The United Methodist Church. The WCC has been present at every climate change conference since 1992, advocating for climate justice.[34]

In addition to faith-based organizations, the global movement for climate justice includes interest groups and communities of every kind.

Around the world, small, local, human-scaled groups are joining together for education and action on these issues. In turn, these coalitions are forming networks across demographics and borders, and taking coordinated actions that demonstrate hope for systemic transformation.

Indigenous Networks

Idle No More is a global indigenous rights movement that originated in Canada, where the extraction of oil from tar sands is destroying the land and livelihood of native people.[35] People around the world are supporting this movement, which is dedicated to protecting indigenous sovereignty and the rights of the earth. Indigenous communities today are at the forefront of struggles to prevent the ever-increasing extraction of fossil fuels that produce climate change.

The United Methodist Church has long upheld the rights of indigenous peoples. The treaty rights of indigenous people throughout North and South America have repeatedly been violated by oil, gas, mining, and energy companies that pollute traditional lands, which have sustained native peoples for millennia.[36] Indigenous leaders are calling for support in their struggles to prevent the pollution of their air, land, and water by dirty extraction technologies. Idle No More, the Indigenous Environmental Network,[37] and other groups that support indigenous rights also challenge us to honor creation by respecting the rights of the earth.

Youth Leadership

Young people around the world are rising up and taking on leadership roles in the movement for climate justice. College students are at the forefront of the movement to divest from fossil fuels companies. Many colleges, seminaries, faith communities, foundations, cities, and counties have divested or are in the process of screening out fossil fuels from their investment portfolios.

Young people are also taking a stand through demonstrations and nonviolent direct action to demand strong action on climate change. In 2008, Tim DeChristopher, a young man in his twenties, engaged in an act of civil resistance by bidding on several parcels of pristine Utah lands that were being auctioned off to oil and gas companies. The auction itself was later ruled to be illegal. Nevertheless, DeChristopher served twenty months in federal prison. After he was released, he co-founded Peaceful Uprising, an organization dedicated to creative nonviolent action for climate justice.[38]

A young woman named Anjali Appadurai delivered a speech in 2011 that transfixed delegates of the Climate Summit in Durban, South Africa. She said, "I speak for more than half the world's population. We are the silent majority. You've given us a seat in this hall, but our interests are not on the table. What does it take to get a stake in this game? Lobbyists? Corporate influence? Money? You have been negotiating all of my life. In that time, you've failed to meet pledges, you've missed targets, and you've broken promises . . . So, distinguished delegates and governments of the developed world: deep cuts now. Get it done."[39]

After rousing applause, most of the delegates took their seats, while fifty young people remained standing. Ms. Appadurai stepped away from the podium, dropped the pages of her speech, and shouted: "Mic check." The young people called back: "Mic check." As she called out each phrase, the youth echoed her words: "Equity now. You've run out of excuses. And we're running out of time. Get it done. Get it done. *Get it done. Get it done.*"[40]

Women as a Powerful Force

Women are also organizing themselves as a powerful force in the struggle for climate justice. In the Global South, women are the primary caretakers of food, water, and fuel for their families and communities. For this reason, women and their dependent children are disproportionately affected as droughts spread, waterways evaporate, and soils dry up.[41] Women and children, particularly girls, also face increased risk in other forms of natural disaster, including extreme weather events that are more likely with climate change.[42]

Women are coming together, locally, regionally, and across continents to form networks of education and action. The Women's Environment and Development Organization (WEDO) has been organizing women for international conferences and actions related to climate change and other environmental challenges since its inception in 1991.[43] The Women's Earth and Climate Action Network (WECAN International) works with women around the world, especially in developing nations, to take actions that foster sustainability and other solutions to the challenge of climate change.[44] WECAN's declaration states: "We are committed to a transition from a future of peril to a future of promise, to rally the women around the world to join together in action at all levels until the climate crisis is solved."

By educating and motivating women to take action, United Methodist Women is part of this worldwide movement. In September 2014, United Methodist Women from around the country traveled to New York City to join the historic Peoples' Climate March, attended by over 400,000 people, including youth, leaders, members of various faith communities, indigenous peoples, women's organizations, labor, environmental, and human rights groups.[45] This is one example of how members of United Methodist Women engage with other groups in coordinated action on climate change.

Another example of coordinated action is the global campaign against the proposed Keystone XL Pipeline, which would carry bitumen, a heavy form of petroleum, from oil sands in Canada to the Gulf of Mexico for export around the world.[46]

Climate scientist James Hansen has said that if the pipeline is approved it will be "game over for the climate."[47] Idle No More, Peaceful Uprising, 350.org, Interfaith Power and Light, and other groups concerned about climate change and the rights of indigenous people have been coordinating actions to prevent this pipeline from being built. The Sierra Club has made its defeat a priority, and for the first time ever it has called on its members to take nonviolent direct action to prevent the construction of the Keystone XL Pipeline.[48]

As United Methodist Women members, we can join together with other people around the world to support those who are most vulnerable to climate change and who are on the front lines of the struggle for climate justice. Only a global people's movement will have the power to reverse the current course, reveal the bankruptcy of the current system, and lay the foundations for its transformation.

Hope for the Future

As we join together with each other in our local United Methodist Women groups, congregations, annual conferences, denominational gatherings, and with interfaith allies, we bring blessings of faith, alternative values, and spiritual power that help to create the cultural shift that is needed. As we respond to the voices of women and youth, indigenous peoples, people from island nations, and others who suffer "first and worst" from climate change, we recognize the systemic changes that need to be made for the sake of those who are most vulnerable today, for future generations, and for the interconnected web of life. As we join together in the work of climate justice, we become part of a global movement of people working for peace, justice, and the healing of creation.

Surely God is at work through us as we undertake the challenge of creation care ministries. Giving up hope is not an option. The beleaguered

Be Just. Be Green.
Using the 13 United Methodist Women Principles

Principle 1: Accessibility
Ask if your meeting venue complies with the Americans with Disabilities Act (ADA), and ask the facility manager to show you how during your site inspection. When surveying meeting space possibilities, make sure rooms are accessible to people with disabilities.

Principle 2: Affordability
Offer carpooling options for participants in order to provide no- or low-cost transportation options for your event.

Principle 3: Carbon Footprint
Choose a meeting venue that minimizes travel, and encourage carpooling and/or public transportation through your registration process.

Principle 4: Healthy Food and Beverages
Serve fair trade (and organic if possible) tea and coffee at your meeting.

Principle 5: Just Economic Opportunities
Ask vendors, hotels and others you contract with to sign a statement attesting that they do not engage in or benefit from the use of child or slave labor or human trafficking.

Principle 6: Local Solidarity
Use the local solidarity checklist to assess if there are opportunities to be in mission at your event.

Principle 7: Multigenerational Inclusion
Offer child care to participants, making sure that at least two unrelated adults are present at all times with the children.

Principle 8: Paper Use
Ensure any printed items are double-sided and duplicated on paper made with post-consumer recycled content.

Principle 9: Racial Justice
Include a statement in your contracts, speaker agreements, attendee code of conduct, and, if relevant, exhibitor terms and conditions that expresses your intention to host an event that combats all forms of racism and oppression.

Principle 10: Toxin Reduction
Be creative and wise about nametags. Invite participants to bring their own nametag (reusing one they already have). If you are supplying nametags, if possible reuse ones you already have. Be careful of the use of ribbons and other petroleum-based enhancements. If you need to buy more, choose a type that does not use PVC and eliminates unnecessary components like holders and pouches. Encourage attendees to turn in their name badge for reuse.

Principle 11: Waste Reduction
Choose a meeting venue that provides recycling for plastic, paper, glass, and metal.

Principle 12: Water Use
Avoid or eliminate the use of individual bottled water. Encourage attendees to bring their own bottle for refilling and provide pitchers of water or bubblers and promote use of water fountains.

Principle 13: Well-being of Participants
Provide a quiet space for meditation and prayer at the event. This may be a physical space and/or formal times on the agenda that are set aside for this kind of activity.[49]

and suffering peoples of the world are calling us, future generations are calling us, other species facing extinction are calling us. Through all these voices God is calling us to allow the good work already begun in us to be brought to completion, as we allow Christ to live in us and God to work through us for the sake of the whole creation.

Now, to the one who by the power at work within us is able to accomplish abundantly far more than all we can ask or imagine, to that one be glory in Christ Jesus and in the church and in the world to all generations, forever and ever. Amen. (Ephesians 3:20–21). ❂

Global Climate Stewardship

"We acknowledge the global impact of humanity's disregard for God's creation. Rampant industrialization and the corresponding increase in the use of fossil fuels have led to a buildup of pollutants in the earth's atmosphere. These greenhouse gas emissions threaten to alter dramatically the earth's climate for generations to come with severe environmental, economic, and social implications. The adverse impacts of global climate change disproportionately affect individuals and nations least responsible for the emissions. We therefore support efforts of all governments to require mandatory reductions in greenhouse gas emissions and call on individuals, congregations, businesses, industries, and communities to reduce their emissions."[50]

Endnotes

1. "Worship and Global Warming," General Board of Discipleship, accessed May 20, 2015, www.gbod.org/lead-your-church/general-information/resource/worship-and-global-warming.

2. Ibid.

3. Ibid.

4. "Climate Change and Environmental Justice," United Methodist Women, accessed May 20, 2015, www.unitedmethodistwomen.org/what-we-do/service-and-advocacy/mission-focus-issues/environmental-justice.

5. "How Cool is Your Congregation?" Interfaith Power and Light, accessed May 20, 2015, www.coolcongregations.org/calculator.

6. Homepage, Carbonfund.org, accessed May 20, 2015, www.carbonfund.org.

7. Duncan Clark, "A complete guide to carbon offsetting," The Guardian, September 16, 2011, www.theguardian.com/environment/2011/sep/16/carbon-offset-projects-carbon-emissions.

8. "Climate Change and Environmental Justice," United Methodist Women, accessed May 20, 2015, www.unitedmethodistwomen.org/what-we-do/service-and-advocacy/mission-focus-issues/environmental-justice.

9. Homepage, God's Renewed Creation: Call to Hope and Action, accessed May 20, 2015, http://hopeandaction.org/main.

10. "God's Renewed Creation: Call to Hope and Action," YouTube video 4:41, posted by DebraS3786, February 12, 2010, https://www.youtube.com/watch?v=Vmo5A1l21Vw.

11. Council of Bishops of The United Methodist Church, "God's Renewed Creation: Call to Hope and Action," Pastoral Letter, November 4, 2009, http://hopeandaction. org/main/wp-content/uploads/2010/03/ Pastoral-Letter-Eng-Handout-2-col.pdf.

12. Wayne Rhodes, "Faith Groups Promote Climate Justice," General Board of Church and Society, December 5, 2014, http://umc-gbcs. org/faith-in-action/faith-groups-promote-climate-justice.

13. Homepage, General Board of Church and Society, accessed May 20, 2015, http://umc-gbcs.org.

14. Homepage, Creation Justice Ministries, accessed May 20, 2015, www.creationjustice.org.

15. Susan Kim, "Climate Change Has Become a Disaster," United Methodist Committee on Relief, April 15, 2014, www.umcor.org/ UMCOR/Resources/News-Stories/2014/ April/0415climatechangebecomesdisaster.

16. David Tereshcuk, "Vulnerable Islands Get Vital Prepping," United Methodist Committee on Relief, March 19, 2012, www.umcor. org/UMCOR/Resources/News-Stories/2012/ March/Vulnerable-Islands-Get-Vital-Prepping.

17. Jacob Chamberlain, "21st Century's First Decade Saw Doubling of Greenhouse Gas Emissions: IPCC," Common Dreams, April 11, 2014, www.commondreams.org/ headline/2014/04/11-5.

18. "About Fossil Free," Fossil Free, accessed May 20, 2015, http://gofossilfree.org/ about-fossil-free.

19. *The Book of Discipline of the United Methodist Church*, "Socially Responsible Investments," ¶717, 528.

20. Chris Tackett, "Bill McKibben on Climate: 'You need to do more than change light bulbs. You need to change the system,'" Treehugger, April 17, 2013, www.treehugger. com/climate-change/bill-mckibben-fossil-fuel-resistance-you-need-do-more-change-light-bulbs-you-need-change-system.html.

21. Mark Fischetti, "Was Typhoon Haiyan a Record Storm?" *Scientific American* blog, November 12, 2013, http://blogs. scientificamerican.com/observations/ 2013/11/12/was-typhoon-haiyan-a-record-storm.

22. "Support for Yeb Sano's hunger strike snowballs," ABS-CBN News, November 20, 2013, www.abs-cbnnews.com/focus/11/20/13/ support-yeb-sanos-hunger-strike-snowballs.

23. "Developing Countries Express Reservations Over IPCC Report," Third World Network, April 17, 2014, www.twn.my/title2/climate/ info.service/2014/cc140405.htm.

24. *The Book of Discipline of the United Methodist Church*, "The Natural World, Global Climate Stewardship," 160 I. (Nashville: Abingdon Press, 2012), 107.

25. Homepage, Citizens Climate Lobby, accessed May 20, 2015, http://citizensclimatelobby.org.

26. "Bill McKibben to Obama: Say No to Big Oil," by Bill Moyers, February 7, 2014, http://billmoyers.com/episode/bill-mckibben-to-obama-say-no-to-big-oil.

27. Homepage, 350.org, accessed May 20, 2015, 350.org.

28. Homepage, Climate Reality Project, accessed May 20, 2015, climaterealityproject.org.

29. Homepage, Climate Justice Now, accessed May 20, 2015, www.climate-justice-now.org.

30. Homepage, Greenfaith, accessed May 20, 2015, http://greenfaith.org.

31. Homepage, Earth Ministry, accessed May 20, 2015, http://earthministry.org.

32. Homepage, Interfaith Power and Light, accessed May 20, 2015, www.interfaith powerandlight.org.

33. Homepage, National Religious Partnership for the Environment, accessed May 20, 2015, www.nrpe.org.

34. "Minute on Climate Justice," World Council of Churches, November 8, 2013, www. oikoumene.org/en/resources/documents/ assembly/2013-busan/adopted-documents-statements/minute-on-climate-justice.

35. Homepage, Idle No More, accessed May 20, 2015, www.idlenomore.ca.

36. Clayton Thomas-Muller, "Energy Exploitation on Sacred Native Lands," *Reimagine: Race, Poverty, and the Environment* (winter 2005/2006), http://reimaginerpe.org/ node/307.

37. Homepage, Indigenous Environmental Network, accessed May 20, 2015, www.ienearth. org.

38. Homepage, Peaceful Uprising, accessed May 20, 2015, www.peacefuluprising.org.

39. Anjali Appadurai, "Youth Speech to the United Nations Framework Convention on Climate Change, COP 17," Durban, South Africa, December 9, 2011, www.coa.edu/assets/news/ anjali%20appadurai%202011%20durban%20 unfccc%20cop%2017.pdf.

40. Ibid.

41. "Women at the Forefront," *Climate Change Connections*, United Nations Population Fund (UNPF) and Women's Environment and Development Organization (WEDO), 2009, www.unfpa.org/sites/default/files/ pub-pdf/climateconnections_1_overview.pdf.

42. "Gender, equity and human rights," World Health Organization, accessed May 20, 2015, www.who.int/gender-equity-rights/en.

43. "Our Story," Women's Environmental and Development Organization, accessed May 20, 2015, www.wedo.org/about/our-story.

44. Homepage, Women's Earth and Climate Action Network, International, accessed May 20, 2015, http://wecaninternational.org.

45. Daquel Harris, "Marching in the Light of God," United Methodist Women, September 23, 2014, www.unitedmethodistwomen.org/ news/marching-in-the-light-of-god.

46. "Keystone XL Pipeline," Friends of the Earth, accessed May 20, 2015, www.foe.org/ projects/climate-and-energy/tar-sands/ keystone-xl-pipeline.

47. James Hansen, "Game Over for the Climate," *The New York Times*, May 9, 2012, www.ny-times.com/2012/05/10/opinion/game-over-for-the-climate.html?_r=0.

48. "Sierra Club, Allies, Engage in Historic Act Civil Disobedience to Stop Keystone XL," Sierra Club, February 13, 2013, http:// content.sierraclub.org/press-releases/ 2013/02/sierra-club-allies-engage-historic-act-civil-disobedience-stop-keystone-xl.

49. "Using the 13 United Methodist Women Principles," United Methodist Women, accessed May 20, 2015, http://www. unitedmethodistwomen.org/what-we-do/ service-and-advocacy/mission-focus-issues/environmental-justice/ sustainability/13-steps.

50. *The Book of Discipline of the United Methodist Church*, "The Natural World, Global Climate Stewardship," 160 D. (Nashville: Abingdon Press, 2012), 107.

About the Author

The Reverend Sharon Delgado is an ordained United Methodist minister, founder and executive director of Earth Justice Ministries, and author of *Shaking the Gates of Hell: Faith-Led Resistance to Corporate Globalization*. She travels widely, leading seminars and workshops and speaking before spiritual communities and secular audiences on issues related to globalization, climate change, economic and environmental justice, and peacemaking, while pointing in the direction of hope and action. She has had many articles published on these themes.

Other Resources from United Methodist Women

Climate Justice in Spanish
Edited by Pat Watkins
ISBN: 978-1-940182-29-2
M3267
$10

Climate Justice in Korean
Edited by Pat Watkins
ISBN: 978-1-940182-30-8
M3266
$10

Climate Justice, Kindle version
Edited by Pat Watkins
ISBN: 978-1-940182-31-5
$5.35

response magazine, April 2016, focusing on climate justice

Place your order with:
United Methodist Women Mission Resources
1-800-305-9857

Climate Justice web page:
www.unitedmethodistwomen.org/climate-justice-study